I0471226

# OUTRAGEOUS
# WEDDING
# ANNOUNCEMENTS

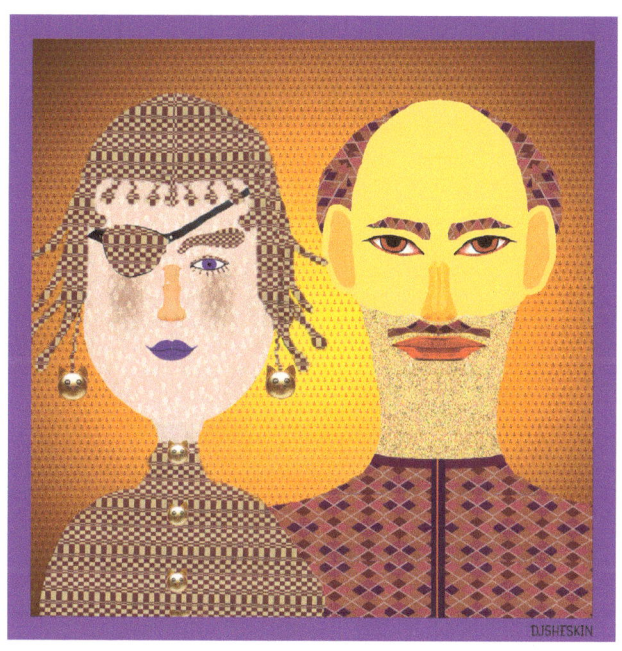

## WRITTEN AND ILLUSTRATED BY

# DAVID SHESKIN

WingSpan Press

Copyright © 2023 by David Sheskin

All rights reserved.

This book is a work of fiction. Names, characters, settings and incidents are either the product of the author's imagination or used fictitiously. Any resemblance to actual events, settings or persons, living or dead, is entirely coincidental.

No part of this book may be reproduced or transmitted in any form or by any means, electronic or mechanical, including photocopying, recording or by any information storage and retrieval system, without written permission from the author, except for the inclusion of brief quotations in reviews.

(Six of the announcements in this book have previously been published online in *The Satirist*.)

Published in the United States and the United Kingdom by WingSpan Press, Livermore, CA

The WingSpan name, logo and colophon are the trademarks of WingSpan Publishing.

ISBN 978-1-63683-042-1 (pbk.)
ISBN 978-1-63683-967-7 (ebk.)

First edition 2023

Printed in the United States of America

www.wingspanpress.com

# Table of Contents

# Introduction

Not so long ago, looking for relaxation and a bit of entertainment, I found myself in my local library reading the wedding announcements in the Styles section of the Sunday New York Times. It soon became apparent to me that attempting to get one's nuptials listed entails becoming a participant in some bizarre social competition in which there are only a handful of winners — more often than not, the latter being people who have a patrician social pedigree or those with exemplary or (on occasion, uncommonly unique) academic or professional credentials.

Inspired by the prosaic descriptions of the couples in the Times this book is comprised of 35 *outrageous* wedding announcements that one is not likely to find in the New York Times or, for that matter, any other newspaper. Each of the announcements begins with a fanciful illustration of the bride and groom followed by biographical information on the couple and their parents. The latter employs an irreverent brand of humor that aspires to depict the evolving realities and absurdities of the gluten free, pan seared, pansexual, politically correct age we live in today.

# Fern Fricassee and Ian Barbecue

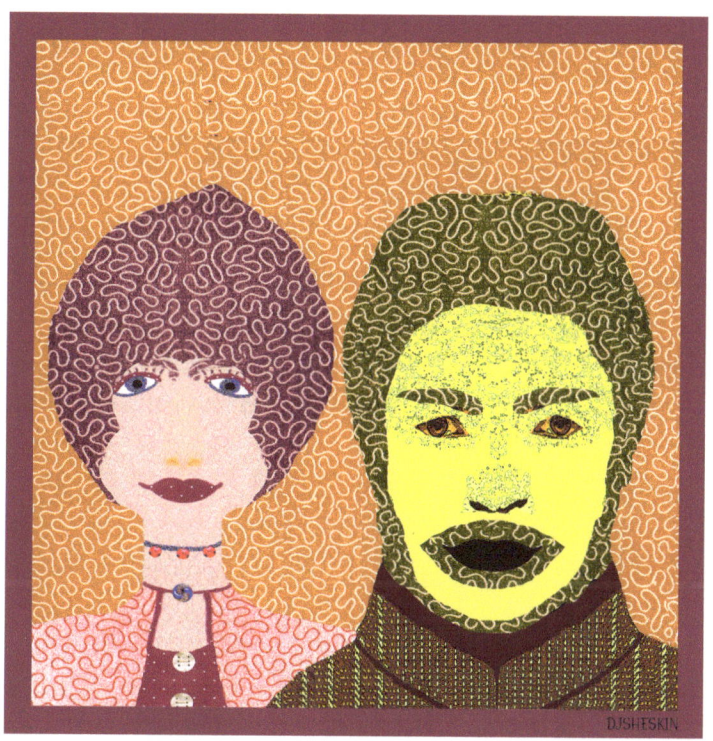

Fern Fricassee and Dr. Ian Barbecue were married March 21 at the Chapel of Blessed Bean Sprouts in Cauliflower, Colorado. High Priestess Indira Ovo-Vegan, a friend of the couple and a mentor of the bride, performed a multinutrient ceremony in a garden overflowing with organic fruits and vegetables incorporating vegetarian, macrobiotic and gluten free elements in the couple's vows.

Ms. Fricassee, 30, has a bachelor's degree in chicken stocks from the Henhouse Institute of Business and Finance in Cockadoodledoo, California. She also holds certificates in roosterology and pullet propriety from Cluck-Cluck University in Poultryville, Pennsylvania. She is fluent in Pig Latin and is an occasional visiting instructor in the latter language at the University of Trash and Garbage in Landfill, Pig Latvia. Ms. Fricassee is a certified soup simmerer and skim milker at Emulsified Farms, in Amuse Boche, Arkansas, a vegan food cooperative that distributes food to reformed alcoholics and suicidal poets.

The bride is the daughter of the late Frances Fricassee and Father Francis Fricassee of Deep-Fried, Nevada. The bride's mother was an éclair and eggnog trader on the Hong Kong stock exchange, as well as a certified kneader and emulsifier at the Institute of Marinating and Maceration in Caramelize, Utah. The bride's father, who was ordained as a Franciscan brother in 2011, is a part-time ascetic, who when not contemplating and meditating, raises hormone free pigs for organ transplantation in humans, He is a former actor who was acclaimed for playing part of Sauté in the Emmy award winning television show "The Parboiled Pimp," and was also nominated for an Academy Award for best actor for the role of Julienne Dollop in the movie "Pan Seared Souls."

Dr. Barbecue, 28, graduated from Gristle College in Porkpie, Georgia with a bachelor's degree in trichinosis. He has a master's degree in bacon and eggs from the Pigpen Culinary Institute and a doctoral degree in Pig Latin from the Oink-Oink Institute of Technology in Hamhock, Iowa. At the present time he is a Pig Latin translator for the Republic of Pig Latvia at the United Nations.

He is the son of Donna Barbecue and Dr. Milton Barbecue of Austin, Texas. His mother retired in 2000 as chief aesthetician, with a specialty in nose hair trimming and ear hair styling, at the Institute for Advanced Study in Princeton, New Jersey. For 20 years she was a professional arm wrestler, and between 1988 and 1994 held the world woman's lightweight right-handed arm wrestling title. At the present time she is employed by the Department of Health and Human Services of the city of Austin where she teaches ligament-friendly arm wrestling to carpal tunnel survivors. The groom's father is a psychologist in private practice who specializes in counseling alien abductees and bee sting survivors. He is the founder and director of Brain and Bowel Cleanse, an annual therapeutic whitewater rafting experience in the Grand Canyon designed for those who have lost family members to food borne illnesses such as E. coli, botulism, listeria and salmonella.

The couple met when the groom was eating in the same restaurant as the bride and had occasion to perform a Heimlich maneuver on her date who at the time had a chicken bone lodged in his throat.

# Paulette Dutkus and Alexander McBride

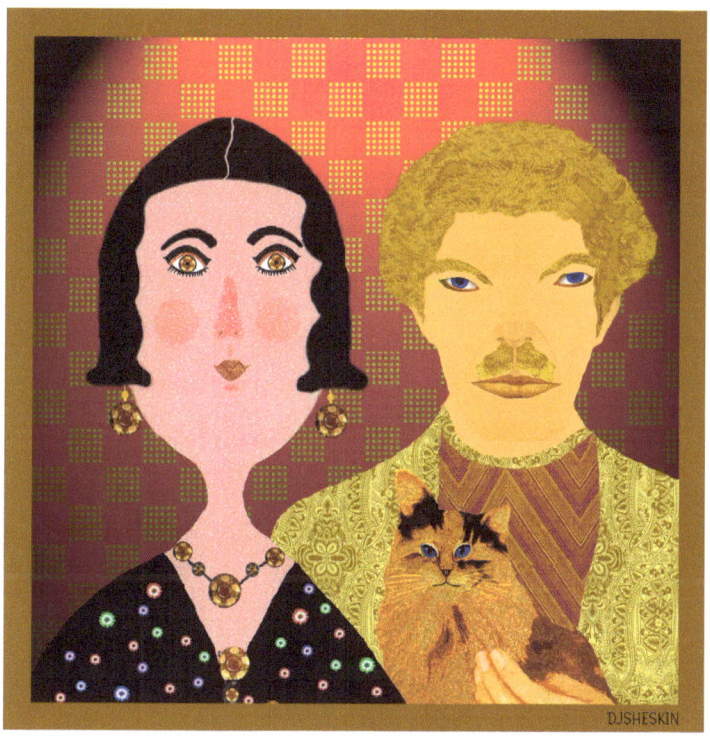

$P$aulette Pearl Dutkus and Alexander Graham McBride were married November 29 on the front steps of the Sigmund Freud Museum in Vienna, Austria. Dr. Armond Schell, President of the International Psychoanalytic Society, conducted a nondenominational ceremony in which the groom read excerpts from Sigmund Freud's "Civilization and Its Discontents" and the bride read the last three pages of Anna Freud's "The Ego and the Mechanisms of Defense."

The couple were introduced to one another three years ago by their surviving biological parents at the Institute for Genetic Exploration in Berkeley, California where they were informed that they had been cloned from the other person's deceased opposite sex parent.

The bride, 21, is a clone of the groom's late mother Miranda McBride, who died in 1997. Ms. Dutkus has a bachelor's degree in mirages and optical illusions from the Floating University of Arts and Science, which sits atop the Grand Canal in Venice, Italy. In the fall she will matriculate at Eros College in Lucerne, Switzerland and begin studying for a doctoral degree in genital arts, with a specialization in castration anxiety and penis envy.

The bride is the daughter of Serena Dutkus of Madison, Wisconsin and the late Mitchel Dutkus. The bride's mother, who claims to have X-ray vision, is an imaging savant at The Hospital of Visionary Medicine in Madison. The bride's late father died at the 1996 Super Bowl in Tempe, Arizona when he was struck on the head by an errant drone that crashed into the stands during the halftime show. Prior to his death Ms. Dutkus's father was the Dean of the School of Tongue Twisters at Peter Piper University in Woodchuck, Wisconsin.

The groom, 22, is a clone of the bride's late father Mitchel Dutkus. Mr. McBride is employed by Journal of The International Psychoanalytic Society to write adulatory obituaries for formerly disgraced members of the psychoanalytic community and to review movies that depict practitioners of psychoanalysis as social deviants. The groom has a bachelor's degree in free association and dream condensation from The Institute of Object Relations in Geneva, Switzerland. Mr. McBride has made public the fact that for the past six years he has had a stiff neck that makes it excruciatingly painful if not impossible for him to engage in any form of sexual activity.

The groom is the son of the late Miranda McBride and Stephen McBride of Salzburg, South Dakota. Before her death, the groom's mother was an award winning school crossing guard who was always assigned to police the most dangerous intersections in Salzburg and the surrounding communities. She was fatally injured in 1997 during a vacation with her husband on the French Riviera when she was impaled by a runaway beach umbrella. The groom's father is the Anna Freud Professor of Oedipal Science at the Institute of Catharsis and Countertransference in Salzburg, South Dakota. He is also the owner of a private gentlemen's club in Salzburg that caters to the needs of individuals who were deprived of oral gratification during childhood.

# Gertrude Mackey and Gilbert Teal

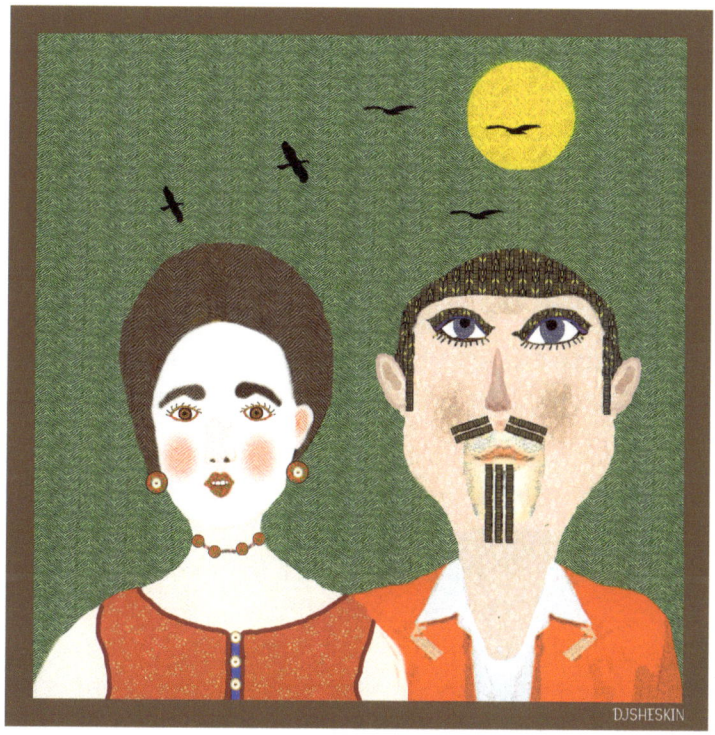

In a hastily arranged marriage by the mothers of the bride and groom, Gertrude Pearl Mackey and Gilbert Albert Teal were joined in holy matrimony September 11 at the Asbestos and Pollen Free Nature Center in Butternut, Vermont. Erin Pollen Mackey, who was ordained as an interfaith deaconess for the day and who for 47 years was the life partner of the bride's late paternal grandfather, officiated the event aided by the vegan priestess Lima Lily Bean, who intermittently interjected chemical free herbivorous bits of wisdom into the couple's vows.

The bride, 46, has an associate of vegan studies degree from the University of Sprouts and Chickpeas in Fiber Springs, Pennsylvania. She is the owner of Tofu Tigers and Lentil Lions, a boutique vegan pastry shop that, among other things, bakes hormone free realistic looking animal crackers that don't bite (unless provoked). Ms. Mackey refers to herself as a "VegVag," since during even numbered months of the year she adheres to a strict vegetarian diet, while during the odd months she is vegan. The bride attributes her inability to find a man with whom to share her life outside the confines of an arranged marriage to the fact that she has a peculiar eccentricity that causes her to yodel whenever she sees or senses that a male has an erection.

Ms. Mackey is the daughter of Hortense and Jerimiah Mackey of Bulger, Vermont. The bride's mother owns Fabric Feet, the only company in New England that makes replacement Velcro toes for people who have lost a digit to frostbite. She also is a freelance designer of flavored, psychedelic, musical shoelaces that she sells online to the rich and famous. Ms. Mackey's father is a rurally licensed dirigible and hot air balloon inflator. He is also a regular participant in asbestos abatement competitions — an increasingly popular yet hazardous sport in which two or more teams not wearing any protective gear vie against one another in an asbestos filled environment to determine which team is most efficient in eliminating all traces of silicate minerals.

Ms. Mackey's late paternal grandfather, Robert Mackey, was the only person to have ever served as the United States Ambassador to Easter Island. He is, however, best remembered for the fact that on his 45th birthday during a beard growing competition he was struck by a bolt of lightning, and from that point forward became psychic to the degree that he was able to foresee the day (but not circumstances) of his own death as a result of him breaking his neck by tripping over his beard, which happened to be 8 feet long.

The groom, 57, is the head bellhop at the Plaza Hotel in New York City. He is a former valedictorian of the Academy of Baggage and Luggage in Manhattan, where for the past 27 years he has been a member of the faculty teaching courses in The History of Bellhopping in Europe and North America, Duffle bag Physics, Suitcase and Backpack Science, and Everything You Wanted to Know but Were Afraid to Ask about Hotel Tipping. Over the years, the groom has mentored over 500 bellhops and received numerous awards for his handling of paraphernalia, and is especially revered in the hospitality industry for his exceptional skills at maneuvering wheeled aluminum and polycarbonate suitcases. Mr. Teal attributes his inability to find a woman with whom to share his life outside the confines of an arranged marriage to the fact that he is afflicted with a rare and undiagnosed medical condition that periodically causes him to have unpredictable episodes of frantic burping and farting.

The groom is the son of Mina and Asa Teal of Kidney Bean, Vermont. The groom's mother is a skilled animal prosthetist whose practice focuses on constructing replacement pods for snails and turtles that have lost their shells due to disease or have come out on the short end of an interspecies altercation. The groom's father, who in spite of being a devout Christian, is the only insurance broker in Vermont who will sell an atheist insurance against an act of God.

The groom's late maternal grandfather, Umberto Orosco, was an esteemed Italian tailor who in 1978 created the world's longest zipper that when extended to its full length of 403 kilometers stretched from Genoa, Italy to Marseilles, France.

The couple was introduced to one another for the first time in the parking lot of the wedding venue one half hour before the blessed event. Accompanied by their mothers, they will honeymoon at The Vegetable Stock Passion Pantry and Spa, a nondenominational vegan resort in Fallow Fields, Ireland that, in addition to supplying guests with videos on coital logistics, provides optional kosher meals and onsite mental health counseling.

# Bette Bo Ling Bong and Corey Calvin Cockatoo

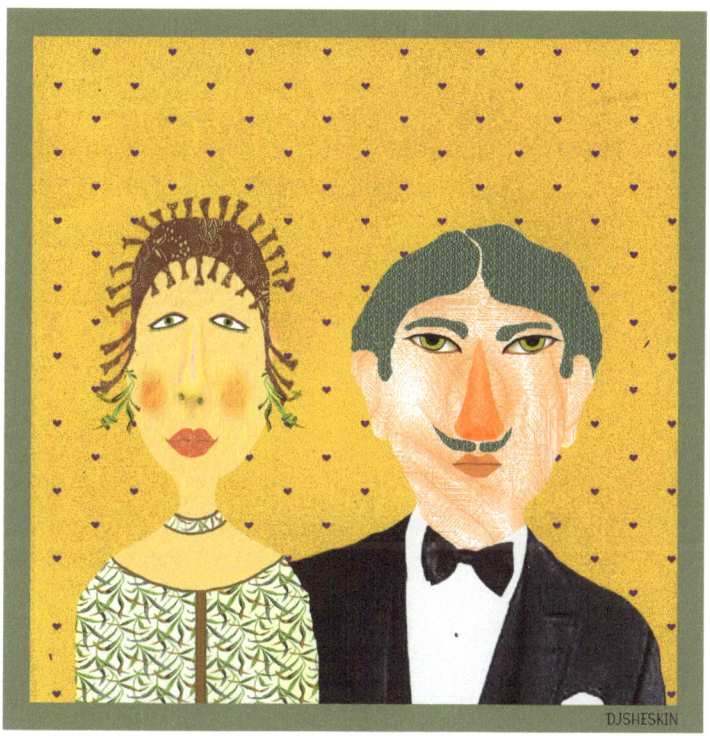

**B**ette Bo Ling Bong and Corey Calvin Cockatoo were married January 1 at the Islington, Idaho Marriage Bureau. The Honorable Huffington O'Crudite, a staff member of the City Clerk's Office officiated. On Dec. 8, Rabbi Jeffery Mohel and Father Andrew Sin will lead the couple in an exchange of interdenominational vows at the Purgatory Chapel in Myagas, Paraguay.

Ms. Bong, 26, is a former adult film performer who participated in over 30 X-rated movies. She is also the chair of the Young Ladies Etiquette Cooperative in Mataplan, North Dakota. She is a licensed breeder of hookworms and pinworms, and is currently a student at the University of Idaho with a double major in alien anthropology and Victorian etiquette. She already holds a degree in forensic cooking from The National University of Mexico.

She is the daughter of Li Li Wang Kvetch Bong and Dr. Raphael F Bong of Coldsore, Georgia. The bride's father, a native of mainland China, achieved the rank of colonel in the Army of the People's Republic of China, and was the recipient of two Purple Pandas, the second highest honor awarded in the Chinese militia. Upon emigrating to the United States in 1972 Dr. Bong assumed a position as a pediatric psychoanalyst at the Center for Neonatal Psychiatry in Atlanta, Georgia where he was employed until last year, when he was fired for refusing to empty a diaper pail. He is currently a senior tattoo artist, specializing in asymmetrical buttock imprints, at Tramp Stamps Designs in Atlanta. The bride's mother is an award winning fortune cookie writer for Feng Shui Productions, whose main offices are in Shanghai, China. Prior to that she was a Tarot card reader and upper level window washer for Nostradamus Prophecies in Beijing.

The groom, 42, has a bachelor's degree in equestrian eurhythmics from Baptist Racetrack Seminary in Louisville, Kentucky, and a master's degree in knitting from the University of Threads in Stringfellow, South Carolina. In 2015 he was awarded a diploma in international intrigue from the French National Intelligence Academy. At the present time Mr. Cockatoo is the lead manager of quality control for Thoroughbred Prophylactics, a Boise, Idaho birth control conglomerate committed to regulating equine reproduction. He is also fellow in the Rocky Mountain chapter of Bobbie's Miracles, a youth charity based in Antarctica that is committed to enhancing the visibility of penguins and aardvarks in the Northern Hemisphere.

Mr. Cockatoo is the son of Frieda Rot Cockatoo and Corey Cockatoo of Munchausen, Mississippi. The groom's mother is a freelance airplane repro person who specializes in reclaiming twin-engine monoplanes. His father is a professional snake milker whose specialty is extracting venom from rattlesnakes and black mambas.

The couple met in 2014 when on a dare from his best friend Mr. Cockatoo traveled to Los Angeles to audition for an X-rated movie. During the audition he was paired with Ms. Bong and it was apparent to everyone on the set that the couple shared a powerful chemistry. To no one's surprise, three months later they became a couple and since then have been inseparable. In 2016 on a vacation trip sponsored by Toxic Treks of Pestilence, Pennsylvania, while outside the condemned nuclear power plant in Chernobyl, Russia Mr. Cockatoo and Ms.

Bong discarded their hazmat suits in order to allow the groom to slip a 1.2 carat diamond ring on the bride's finger. Two weeks later in a condemned landfill chocked full of banned herbicides and pesticides, Mr. Cockatoo persuaded Ms. Bong to retire from the movie industry and accompany him back to Boise to raise parasitic worms and start a family.

# Leola Penelope Puke and Peter Paul Pissant

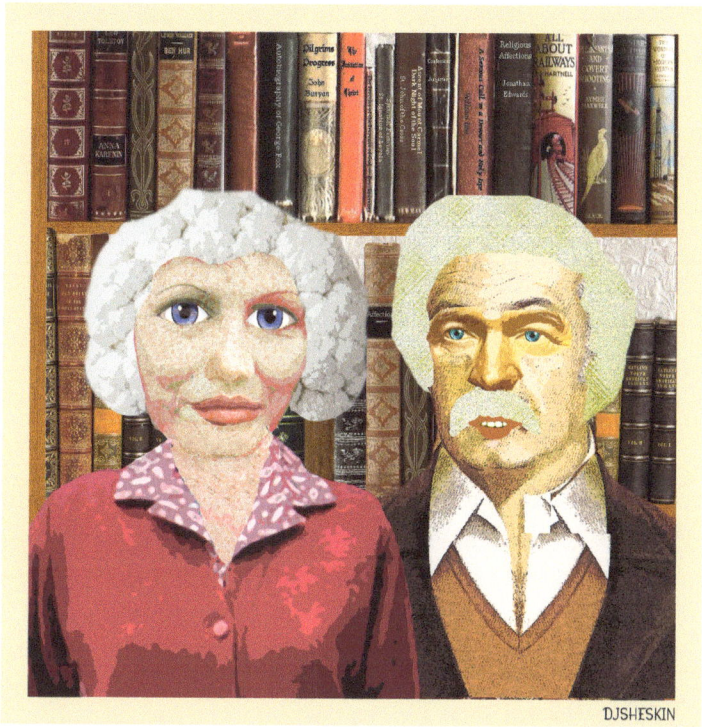

DJSHESKIN

Leola Penelope Puke and Dr. Peter Paul Pissant were married January 17 at Kahana Bay Beach Park, in Kaaawa. Hawaii. The Reverend Debby Douche, a stepsister of the groom and an ordained minister of the Church of Irreligious Pseudoscience, officiated.

Ms. Puke, 69, is the mother of eight adult out of wedlock children, all of whom were remanded to foster care shortly after birth. She is currently executive director for Planned Parenthood in Avarice, Kansas, as well as a freelance midwife, specializing in delivery of breech babies. Ms. Puke has a bachelor's degree in artificial insemination from The Mother of All Mothers University in Chicago and a doctoral degree in junk science from Hazel Crest University, Liege, Belgium. She is an adjunct lecturer in the department of rigor mortis at the University of Unsterile Mortuary Science in Moline, Illinois where she teaches courses in formaldehyde-free embalming and gluten-free cosmetology.

She is the daughter of the late Colonel Pauley Puke, who after serving in the United States military for 28 years became a soldier of fortune participating in numerous international conflicts. After a contentious internationally publicized trial he was found guilty of "Crimes against Humanity," and was executed by a firing squad in 1998 for his activities as a mercenary during civil wars in Sierra Leone, Angola and Rwanda. The bride's mother, Hazel Hanover Puke, also deceased, was the mother of 13 children and a devoted housewife. For 42 years she served as a Boy Scout den mother and a Girl Scout troop mistress, and was the grand prize winner of the Pillsbury Bake-Off a record four times for her recipes for bejeweled cranberry-crab cake, pumpkin ravioli with salted sardine whipped cream, sour dough Oreo MSG free donuts and pepperoni streusel bars with orange-lime filling. She died in 2005 as a result of choking on a slice of deconstructed Apple Brown Betty she was judging during a pastry competition at the Texas State Fair in Dallas.

Mr. Pissant, 64, is a morning news anchor and evening weatherman at WFLOP, with studios in Lincoln, Nebraska and Menopause, Iowa. For the past five years he has been the president of Teeth and Feet without Borders, an international humanitarian organization that promotes foot care and dental hygiene in third world countries. He graduated summa cum laude from Harvard Pacific University with degrees in unnatural international relations and fog and smog. He also has degrees from the Dartmouth School of Podiatry and Alimentary Canals in flatfeet and hiatal hernias.

The groom is the son of Phillipe Pisant of Paris, France and the late Mashishi Pooyarihihosi Pisant of Calcutta, India. The groom's father, now deceased, was an award winning brassiere designer for Christian Dior and Yves Saint Laurent, as well as a professional water polo player who was drowned by an irate opponent during a quarter-final water polo match in the 1992 Barcelona Olympics. The groom's mother is a graduate of Chaudhary Charan Singh Haryana Agricultural University in Hisar, India where she received an advanced degree in irrigation and snow pea pod nutrient management. Subsequent to her graduation she worked as a food taster in penal institutions in the Indian states of Maharashtra and West Bengal. She met her husband in 1981 during a riot at a cricket match in Mumbai. After her husband's death she moved to the United States where for the past 20 years she has worked in Plano, Texas as a snake charmer and carnival barker.

The couple met in the Feet to Face Spa, an all-purpose beauty salon in Waco, Texas, where Dr. Pissant had accompanied his mother for her monthly pedicure. After spotting Ms. Puke having her eyes tweezed he asked if she would accompany him to a roller derby marathon. Although Ms. Puke demurred, she did give him her contact information, and six months later the couple reconnected and bonded largely on the basis of their mutual love of Ceylonese cuisine, waterboarding and the breeding of large rodents — most specifically, pacas and capybaras.

# Samantha Shira Smith and
# Samuel Steven Smith

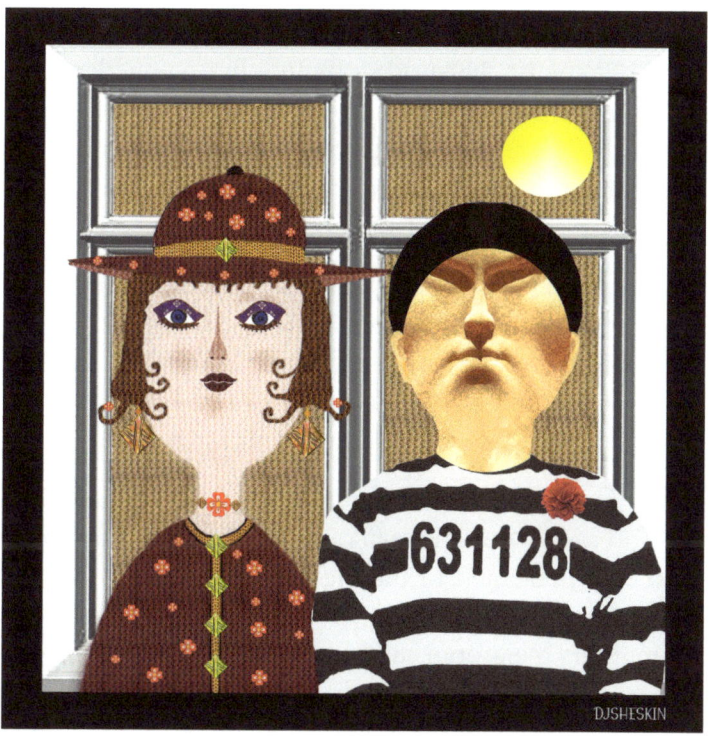

Samantha Shira Smith and Samuel Steven Smith were married February 14 in the Georgia State Penitentiary in Reidsville, Georgia by Warden Samuel Sherwin Smith, the father of the bride, who was ordained as a Universal Life Minister for the event.

The couple met at An Assemblage of Smiths, a semiannual convention of citizens of the Deep South who share the surname Smith.

The bride, 29, graduated magna cum laude from Magdalena University in Managua, Nicaragua from which she received a bachelor's degree in narcissism and a master's degree in fascism. She is currently employed as a senior matchmaker for Enamored with My Image, the leading online matchmaking service for narcissists and fascists. Prior to working as a matchmaker she was a part-time floor waxer and an instructor of mixology at Spigots for Bigots, a coeducational vocational school in Jakarta, Indiana for bartenders and right wing ideologues.

She is the daughter of Samuel Sherwin Smith and Shirley Sidra Smith. The bride's father, who began a career in law enforcement as a correction officer in 1983, has served as the warden of three state and two federal penitentiaries. During that time he has quelled four major riots that have resulted in the deaths of 142 prisoners and 14 correction officers. He is also an avid collector and online dealer of prison memorabilia, specializing in handcuffs and billy clubs. The bride's mother is the president and CEO of We Value Your Time, a company that provides clients who wish to queue up for an event well in advance of its opening with someone to take their place in line. She is the godmother of six children, one of whom is the mistress of the Prime Minister of Luxemburg.

The bride is the granddaughter of General Stephen Samson Smith who was a senior general in the Continental Army during the Revolutionary War. General Smith was one of the original signers of the Declaration of Independence, and also served as Thomas Jefferson's pimp and slave master when the latter was the Governor of Virginia from 1779-1781.

The groom, 54, is a former death row inmate who was granted a new trial in 2013 and is presently free on bail as a result of highly questionable DNA evidence that was presented to the Georgia Supreme Court in 2010 by lawyers from the Innocence Project. During his 34 years of incarceration for multiple murders the groom earned a bachelor's degree in Zen studies, a master's degree in papier mâché and a doctoral degree in eyelash dyeing and eyebrow trimming. He is currently employed as a junior dog groomer at The Rabid Canine dog sanctuary in Drooling Springs, Georgia, as well as being a volunteer youth counselor for Slicing and Dicing, a privately funded philanthropic organization committed to teaching antisocial teens how to use machetes and daggers to defend themselves from the police.

The groom is the son of Samuel Solomon Smith and the late Sylvia Samantha Smith. The groom is the stepson of Susannah Serena Smith. The groom's father is a professional dowser whose specialty is locating decomposed corpses and radioactive waste buried in remote rocky terrain. His father is the author of "The Encyclopedia of Stones, Pebbles and Ossified Mud" (Quicksand Press, 1992). The groom's late mother had a Ph.D. in nuclear physics from the California Institute of Technology. Although the nature of her death was classified by the United States Government, with her file sealed until the year 2150, according to the groom she died in 2003 as a result of radiation poisoning as a result of a nuclear accident in a clandestine nuclear facility located on an island off the coast of Alaska.

Prior to her death the groom's mother also had a business as a taxidermist, with a specialty in stuffing mongooses and pygmy hippopotamuses. The groom's stepmother is a Professor of Gibberish at Balderdash University, in Claptrap, Colorado, as well as being an internationally licensed crab stuffer and hummingbird tamer.

# Amber Lotus and Barbara Sylph

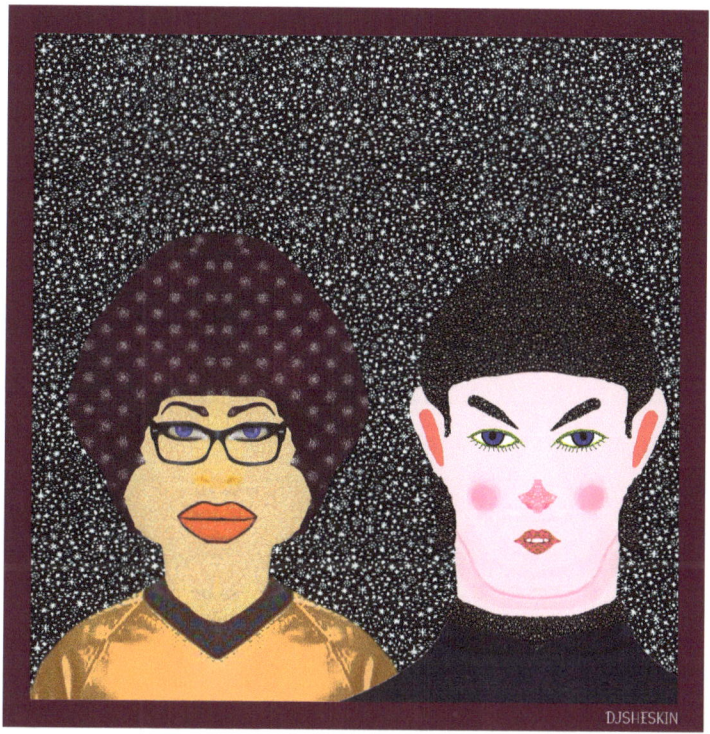

Amber Lotus and Barbara Sylph, two pilgrims who were kidnapped from planet Earth by aliens and transported beyond the Milky Way to spiral galaxies that float along the outer margins of the universe, were married in or around February 18 at an unspecified location in the Andromeda Galaxy. The ceremony was performed by the celebrated octogenarian rabbinical time traveler Whitley Foster Scheweringer, who was aided in leading the couple through their vows by the nomadic universal priestess Pi R Squared who had traveled millions of light years to the event from a planet in the center of the Sombrero Galaxy.

The couple met on an interstellar cruise in which 147 abductees had been invited to tour 16 different galaxies over a distance of 35 million light years. During a stopover in the Pinwheel Galaxy Ms. Lotus, who has spent five and a half years away from Earth, and Ms. Slyph, who has been gone for 22 months, were introduced to one another by the cruise coordinator, and discovered that prior to their abduction they had lived in cities with the same name — Ms. Lotus in Gosford, Alabama and Ms. Sylph in Gosford, Australia. Within the next light year the two "Gosford Gals" (as they were referred to by their fellow abductees) happily discovered that they had finally found their soul mate in, of all places, the remotest regions of outer space.

Prior to her abduction Amber Lotus, 34, was employed by soup manufacturers to design alphabet pasta –specifically, the letters used in alphabet soup. Within both the soup and typography communities she was known for her use of idiosyncratic and sometimes outrageous fonts in her pasta designs. During her time on Earth, Ms. Lotus was also an accomplished wilderness guide who was lauded for her ability to start a fire using dental floss and a toothpick.

Amber Lotus is the daughter of Pilar Lotus of Tucson, Arizona and Sentinel Lotus of Mobile, Alabama. Her mother is a former carousel pony groomer who for the past five years has lived in the Kitt Peak National Observatory in Tucson, Arizona where she has spent the better part of each day peering through a Hiltner 2.4 meter telescope searching for her daughter. Ms. Lotus' father salvages and repairs automobiles that had been submerged in flood waters and rehabilitates them by plugging up holes with chewing gum and camouflaging rust using discarded beauty products such as nail polish, eye liner and lip gloss.

Ms. Sylph, 29, who was raised in a blended family that included four biological siblings, five step siblings, six hamsters, three toucans and an ever changing assortment of amphibians, is an honors graduate of Marsupial University in Wallaby, Australia with a degree in Aboriginal arts. Prior to her abduction she was employed as a boomerang designer by the Kangaroo-Koala Cooperative in Wallaby. She was also a competitive boomerang thrower and currently holds the woman's circular throwing distance record for a 50 gram boomerang.

Barbara Sylph is the daughter of Aurora and Cyrus Sylph of Sydney, Australia. Her mother is an amphibian support tutor who trains frogs, toads, salamanders and newts to become loyal and nurturing companions to dogs and cats who are confined at home alone when their owners leave the house. Ms. Sylph's father is an alien abductee survivor who was kidnapped at the age of 14 and returned 13 years later missing all of his teeth, his lower bowel, his right eyebrow and both pinkie toes. For the past 15 years he has led support groups for other abduction survivors who have experienced amputation and mutilation at the hands of aliens. He also writes poetry about the alien abduction experience and is the author of the chapbook "Ballads and Sonnets from Andromeda and Beyond" (Probe Press, 2005).

# Ginger Nandini Gallstone and Ulysses Karan Ulcer

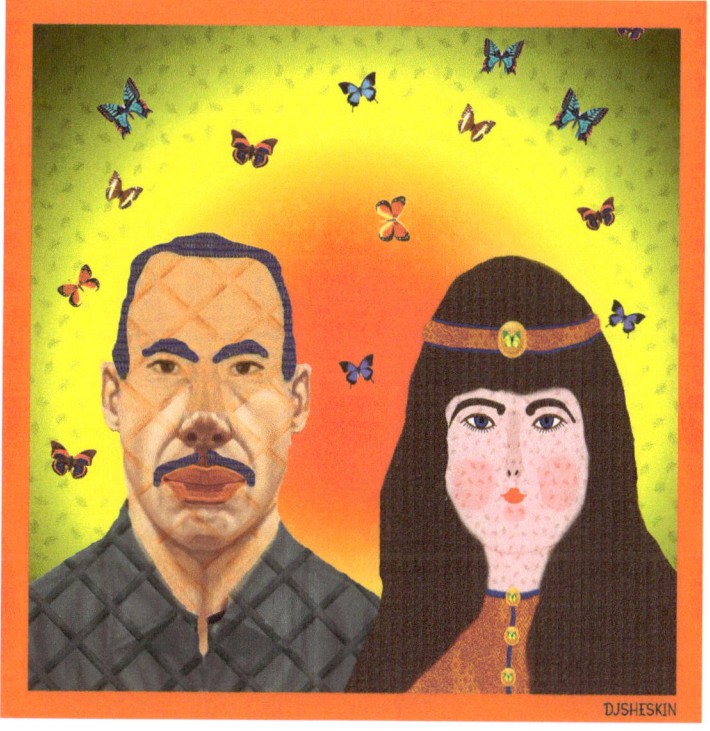

**W**earing oxygen masks, Ginger Nandini Gallstone and Ulysses Karan Ulcer were married February 24 on the summit of Mt. Everest in Nepal at 29.029 feet above sea level with the temperature –30°C. The event was performed by Tenzing Zhumul, a Sherpa with 20 previous ascents to the summit, who was ordained for the event by the Himalayan Hookup Ministries. Two days later with 123 Occidentals and 14 Sherpas in attendance, an interdenominational ceremony serenaded by the Mormon Tabernacle Choir, was held at 17,600 feet at the Everest Base Camp, with Orthodox Jewish Rabbi Edgar Ponsky and Reverend Isaac Gallstone of the Unification Church, who is an uncle of the bride, officiating.

The bride, 29, who for the present will retain her maiden name, graduated at the top of her class from Tip-Top College of Sport Science in Taunggyi, Myanmar with degrees in badminton and ping-pong. She also holds a master's degree in burping and farting from Effluvium Technological Institute in Jeonju, South Korea. Ms. Gallstone currently works as a water slide tester at Disneyland in Anaheim, California and Disney World in Orlando, Florida. She is also employed by the cities of Anaheim and Orlando as an air quality tester and waste facility consultant. For the past ten years the bride has been a professional ping-pong player who has won or placed in 633 international tournaments. She intends to retire from professional ping-pong competition next year, at which time she will assume her husband's surname.

The bride is the daughter of Linda Mallio Mpu and the late Dr. Gregory Gallstone. The bride's father was a cryptozoologist who was credited with sighting 16 thought to be nonexistent or extinct species such as chucapabra, Bigfoot, the Loch Ness monster, pterodactyl and three genus of dinosaurs (brontosaurus, diplodocus and tyrannosaurus). In 2008 he was posthumously inducted in the Truth or Trash Hall of Fame in Hyphenated, Nevada. The bride's mother is a care-taker of a private island off the coast of Taiwan that is owned by Sun Loo-Sing, the fourteenth richest man in the world. To occupy herself on the island, which is only inhabited by herself, three eunuchs and 12 Komodo dragons, she breeds carrier pigeons and miniature schnauzers and edits wonton recipes for The Food Network.

The groom, 34, is a second year resident in urology at the Hindu-Mormon School of Osteopathic Medicine in Yiddish Valley, Utah. He received a bachelor of science degree in cursive graphology and precognition from Edgar Cayce University in Virginia Beach, Virginia. He is certified as a spelunker and cave diver by the National Speleological Society in Huntsville, Alabama, and is only one of only 36 people worldwide to be designated a Master Spelunker by Union Internationale de Spéléologie, the international umbrella organization for caving and speleology. In 2011 he was part of nine nation cave exploration team that broke a world record when it descended to a depth of 2100 meters (6890 feet) in the Krubera-Voroyna cave (considered the Everest of caves) located in Abkhazia in southern Russia near the Black Sea.

He is the son of Ulric Ulcer and Mina Tumeric Ulcer of Edinburgh, Oregon. The groom's father is a deer urine farmer who markets undiluted whitetail pee to deer hunters in the Pacific Northwest. His mother is a free-lance pet food taster, working out of a prefabricated shed on the summit of Mt. Hood, whose specialty is tasting ferret pellets, hamster chow and guinea pig treats.

Ms. Gallstone and Dr. Ulcer met on a spelunking expedition in 2002 when

Dr. Ulcer was employed as a guide by Chill Seekers, an adventure tour vacation business located in Darwin, Australia. They shared their first kiss at a depth of 945 meters (3100 feet) in a frigid underground lake.

Although the couple will reside in Utah until Dr. Ulcer completes his residency, Ms. Gallstone, who is bisexual, will periodically commute to California and Florida to fulfill her professional responsibilities, as well as to continue affairs she is having with two women with whom she has been romantically involved for the past seven years.

# Edie Mourn and Telger Wolffender Berger

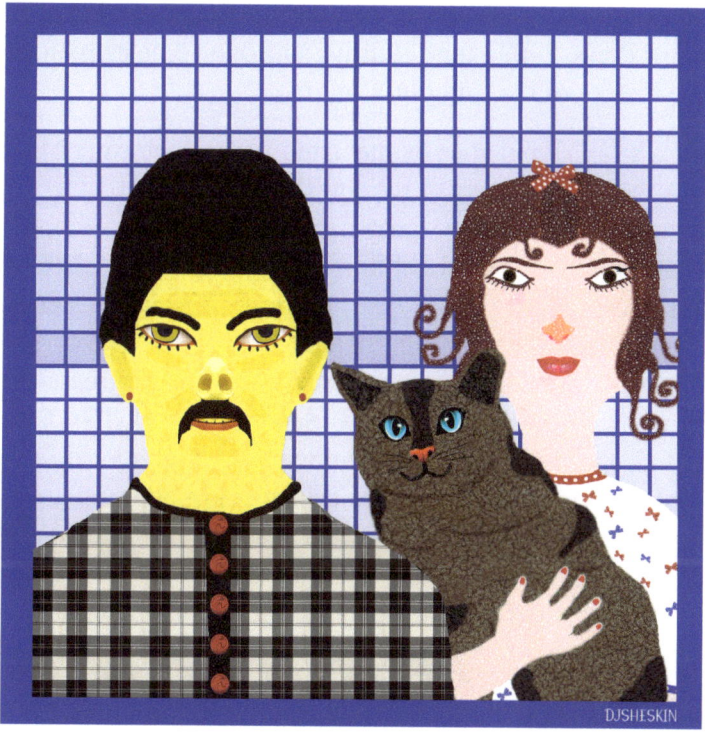

Edie Mourn and Telger Wolffender Berger were married March 13 in a waste disposal plant situated inside a landfill outside of Cape Town, South Africa. Father Oswald Penk, a defrocked Roman Catholic priest, and Dr. Molly Pet, a board certified pediatric podiatrist who was ordained for two hours by the city of Cape Town, officiated.

Ms. Mourn, 34, is a senior porta potty designer for Feces Plus, an international waste technology firm that is credited with installing the first porta potty on the moon in 2016. She graduated cum laude from The Durbin Institute of Technology with a bachelor of science degree in intestinal fortitude and has a master's degree in regurgitation and defecation from the Zimbabwe School of Postprandial Arts.

The bride is the daughter of Monique Elyse of London, England and Dr. Satan Mourn of Belgrave, Bulgaria. Her father is an associate professor of anarchy and insurgency at Arsenic University in Plovdiv, Bulgaria. He is the founder and executive editor of The Annals of Sexual Anarchy, a scholarly journal devoted to the study of unnatural and uncomfortable sexual positions. The bride's mother is an ecclesiastical etiquette consultant who formerly served as an advisor to Pope Benedict XVI regarding matters of civility and decorum. She is the author and illustrator of "Papal Blunders" (Ecclesiastical Press, 2002), the definitive source on embarrassing pontifical gaffes in the history of the Catholic Church.

The groom, who is 32 and goes by the name Wolf, is a former Mr. Universe (2008-2011) who was forced to relinquish his title in 2012 as a result of chronic steroid abuse. For the past decade he has been employed as a fumigator and sterilizer by Blood and Guts, the preeminent crime scene cleaning service in North America. The groom has an associate's degree in bodily fluids and blowflies from Slaughterhouse Institute of Technology in Saskatchewan, Canada and a bachelor's degree in grease and grime removal from the Evangelical Disposal Seminary, in Quebec City. Within his capacity as a crime scene decontaminator, Mr. Berger on at least ten occasions has played a prominent role in rehabilitating environments in which mass murders involving five or more victims occurred. With regard to the latter he has been awarded two Medallions of Excellence by the International Association of Crime and Trauma Rehabilitation.

Mr. Berger is the son of Sparrow Lu Berger, of Qaanaaq, Greenland and Wollfender Berger of Alberta, Canada. The groom's mother is a retired pearl diver who practiced her craft for 27 years in the Sulu Archipelago in the southwestern Philippines and the Gulf of Mannar (between Sri Lanka and India). In 1984 Ms. Lu Berger set a world record for a female diver by holding her breath under water for 11 minutes and 23 seconds. She retired in 1991 as a result of medical problems resulting from multiple episodes of decompression sickness. At the present time she is a dogsled instructor in the Arctic Circle and a docent at the Museum of Dry Ice and Venomous Whale Blubber in Thule, Greenland. Mr. Berger's father, who has a doctoral degree in rubbish and clutter, is the Silas Mariner Professor of Trivia and Minutiae at the Institute of Intellectual Tedium in Alberta. He is an Ebola survivor and the author of the best-selling book "Hemorrhagic Healer" (Platelet Press, 1980), which documents how a blind, agnostic, albino, indigenous Sudanese faith healer miraculously rid him of the deadly disease in 1976 while Mr. Berger was working as a roadkill collector in Nzara, South Sudan.

Ms. Bourn and Mr. Berger first met in 2004 when they were both studying ethics and etiquette at Madame Lavender's School of Deportment, Decency and Metaphysics in Marseilles, France. As the bride recalls, one evening the groom inserted an orange milk chocolate M&M in her left nostril during a game of Scrabble, after which she slapped him in the face and didn't speak to him again until seven years later when they reconnected during a bodybuilding competition in Amsterdam, Holland where Mr. Berger was competing and Ms. Mourn was teaching a class on the relationship between personal hygiene and humming. Six months later Mr. Berger proposed to Ms. Mourn by presenting her with a wedding ring nested in a package of her favorite flavored dark chocolate M&Ms.

# Amy Gooch and Forrest Pell

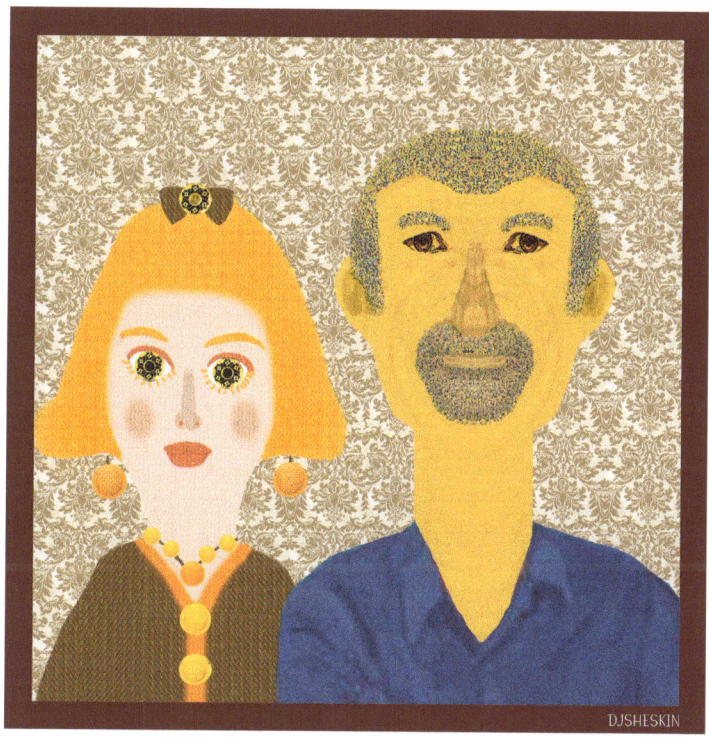

At high noon on the ides of March in a field of wildflowers and chirping crickets, Amy Gooch, an opinionated and rheumy Scorpio who was born under an ascending moon on October 26, 1994, and Forrest Pell, a balding and dyspeptic Sagittarius who was born at sunrise on November 24, 1981, were married beneath an ominous sky filled with cumulus clouds that five minutes into the ceremony poured a torrent of acid rain onto all those who had journeyed to an obscure soybean and tobacco farm outside of Raleigh, North Carolina to partake in a zodiac inspired ceremony authorized by the Church of the Blessed Horoscope. The event was officiated by the articulate, albeit ambivalent, agrarian astrologer Astral Plane, who was aided in leading the couple through their vows by a team of astrological savants who had traveled to the ceremony from each of the seven continents that float atop the oceans of Planet Earth.

The bride, 25, is a peripatetic animal behaviorist who, among other things, has taught every rabbit in Wyoming to line dance and every rattlesnake in Arizona to play chess. She has a bachelor's degree in nonsadistic dominance from the University of Celestial Obedience in Compliance, Minnesota and a master's degree in pseudomasochistic acquiescence from the University of Interplanetary Subservience in Assent, Wisconsin. Ms. Gooch is a lifelong devotee of astrology who at the present time is enrolled in an intensive online program that instructs celestial scholars in the proper care and feeding of hamsters and hedgehogs born under the sun signs of Sagittarius and Libra.

The bride is the daughter of Orchid and Orlando Gooch of Mataplan, New Jersey. Her mother is a former Siamese twin who was attached at the coccyx for 27 years to her identical twin sister Snap Dragon. In 1978 in Yellowkniife, Canada an ethnically diverse team comprised of 11 male, 11 female and two transgender surgeons successfully separated the twins in a marathon 86 hour operation. Orchid Gooch, who along with her sister up to the time of their detachment had taught rehabilitated kleptomaniacs how play mahjong and pinochle, has subsequently become a successful author of 15 best-selling books that document the violent for too many years secret history of Tupperware. The bride's father is a sometimes butcher and baker and full time candle and stick maker. He is the only person in the world known to make scented candles out of human earwax.

The groom, 38, is a professional pole vaulter and master astrologer. He is a former world class pole vaulter who won a silver medal in the 2000 Olympic Games in Sydney, Australia. For the past 14 years he has been employed by the military, law enforcement and, on occasion, private parties, to use his pole vaulting skills to gain access to high-walled compounds that have previously been impervious to penetration. Mr. Pell has a doctoral degree in zodiacal studies from Aquarius University in Taurus, Bulgaria. In 2008 he was certified as a master astrologer by the European Union. At the present time he is under contract with 13 European countries and the United States to conduct astrological readings on suspected spies and political defectors,

The groom is the son on Minerva Pyle of Antibes, France and Derek Pell of Dresden, Germany. His mother is the world's leading authority on the poaching and scrambling of eggs and in the art of hard-boiling an egg to insure seamless removal of the shell. Mr. Pell's father is a law enforcement professional whose specialty is identifying and prosecuting hard-boiled criminals and apprehending individuals involved in poaching African wildlife. He is also a syndicated word scrambler who creates anagrams for newspapers and magazines.

Ms. Gooch and Mr. Pell met on the popular dating app Opinionated and Rheumy Scorpio Looking for a Balding and Dyspeptic Sagittarius.

# Jilly von Stuffenberg and Marcus Aurelius Trumpet

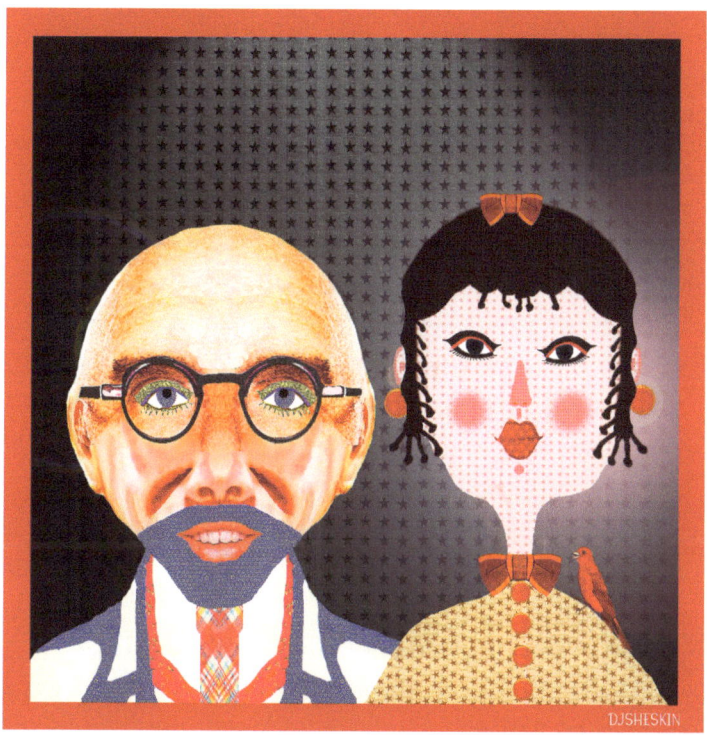

Jilly von Stuffenberg and Marcus Aurelius Trumpet were married March 30 in Gierłoż, Kętrzyn County, Poland (formerly the East Prussian town of Rastenberg) on the site of the former Wolf's Lair, the Eastern Front military headquarters of Adolf Hitler. Webmaster Ian Honeycrisp, an IBM software specialist and Granny Smith Apple polisher ordained for the day by the United Nations Peacekeeping Collective, officiated.

The bride, 41, who is on both the autism and absorption spectrums, is a senior project coordinator for LGBTq Lucifer, a publically funded organization that promotes Devil worship among the sexually disenfranchised regardless of sexuality or gender. Among her professional accomplishments, Ms. von Stuffenberg is credited for coining the term wigotry — which is bigotry against people who design, fit or wear wigs.

The bride is the daughter of the former Hazel Marx and Hienrich Carl von Stuffenberg of Cairo, Illinois. Her mother is a performance artist, who specialties are extracting herself from quicksand. straightjackets, sealed coffins and nasty domestic disputes. She also clones sheep and Shi Tzus and during the Jewish High Holy Days and Valentine's Day serves as a docent at the Museum of Quicksand and Venomous Flora in Cairo, Illinois. The bride's father is a harmonica designer and professional blood donor. From 1988 to 2001 he was a pirouette coach and alternate tenor for the National Academic Bolshoi Opera and Ballet Theater of the Republic of Belarus.

The bride's great grandfather Colonel Clauss von Stuffenberg was executed for his involvement in a plot to assassinate Adolf Hitler at Wolf's Lair on July 20, 1944. Her great grandmother on her mother's side achieved fame in her native Sweden for being an extremely strict and sadistic vegetarian who whipped turnips and smashed potatoes, and whose likeness was published on a 5 kroner ultramarine Swedish postage stamp in 1938, which according to the bride today is valued in the Scott catalog of postage stamps, if mint and in good condition, at $5000.

The groom, 65, is a five time poison ivy survivor. He is a professional bowler who to date has bowled 121 perfect games and 1,222,432 imperfect games. He is also a professional skydiver who has parachuted into 26 active volcanos, 313 inactive volcanos, 126 sinkholes, 43 septic tanks and 14 abandoned oil wells. From 1964 to 1966 Mr. Trumpet was a bat boy for the New York Yankees. His six previous marriages ended in divorce. He has been arrested 17 times for domestic violence, but is proud of the fact that he has never been convicted.

The groom is the son of Isiah "Weiner" Trumpet and the former Margaret Kiera O'Reilly. The groom's father, now deceased, was a hot dog vendor for 48 years at the old Yankee Stadium in the Bronx. His mother, also deceased, cleaned the toilets at the Polo Grounds (the home of the New York Giants) for 39 years. The couple met at an orientation meeting for vendors and cleaners prior to first game of the 1951 World Series between the New York Yankees and New York Giants. On December 6, 1953, two weeks after the birth of her son, the groom's mother revealed to the Archbishop of New York City that during her son's birth while she was in a drug induced twilight sleep she time traveled back into the 14th century where she cut off a lock of Joan of Arc's hair just before she was burned at the stake. She passed the lock of hair on to the Archbishop who sent it to the Vatican where it was kept in storage under lock and key for more than 40 years. In 1996 a Vatican commission authorized by Pope John

Paul II composed of 24 prominent theologians and scientists concluded unequivocally that based on radiocarbon dating, DNA analysis and other sophisticated technology, the hair in question had once belonged to a nineteen year old female who lived during the 14$^{th}$ century.

Ms. von Stuffenberg and Mr. Trumpet met in 2003 on an AARP sponsored tour of World War II battlefields, at which time the groom learned that in 1994 while the bride was vacationing aboard a yacht in the Mediterranean with her then filthy rich friends, she and five other women were captured and held hostage for eight and one-half months by Somalian pirates. To his surprise he discovered that she was liberated one year later by his long time tennis partner and former dermatologist, Dr. Avery Plaque, who at the time was a Lieutenant Commander and a psoriasis counselor in the French Armed Forces serving with the United Nations Expeditionary Forces.

# Freida Coriana Mendoza and Freddy Frack

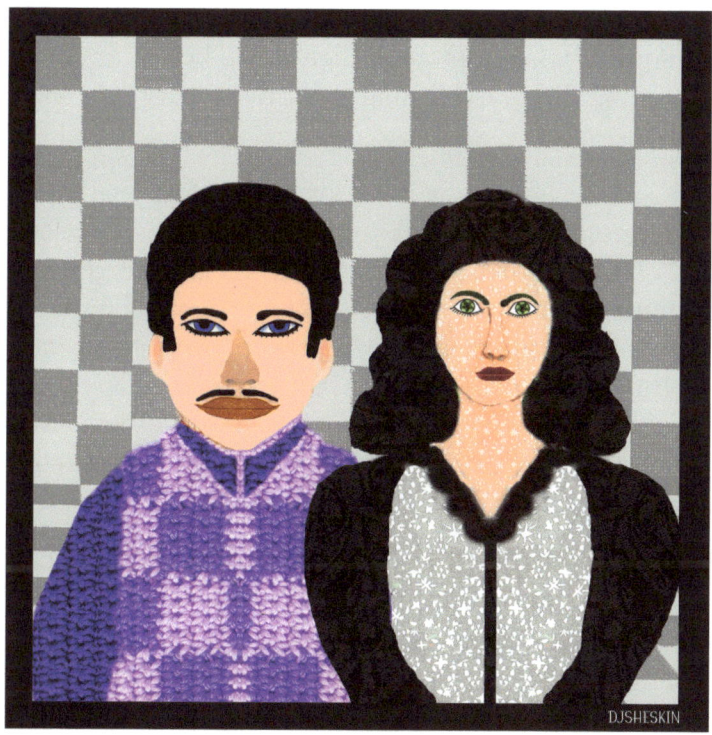

**D**r. Frieda Coriana Mendoza and Freddy Frack were married April 1 in a yurt situated in the Gobi desert 156 miles south of Mandalgobi, Mongolia. Grand Lama Panchen Dorjsuren, a nomadic Buddhist monk who was invited to the event by the father of the bride and who had traveled 2300 kilometers on a camel from Tibet, officiated. After a Buddhist ceremony accompanied by two nomads playing morin khuurs (a bowed two string instrument), the wedding party was fed wild game captured by a golden eagle trained by the renowned Mongolian falconer Batkhuyag Mönkh-Erdene.

The couple first met in June of 2012 in Oxford, England when the groom exposed himself to the bride while she was working on her dissertation on "Human Sexual Perversion" in the Oxford University Library of Arts and Science. Subsequent to his release from a sexual deviation rehabilitation program in 2015 the couple reconnected last year at a swinger's convention in Rabble Hill, Wales. During the interim between her first encounter with the groom and last year, Ms. Mendoza had attended intensive workshops in Nepal and Tibet on forgiveness and empathy where she adopted a new outlook regarding transgression. Because of the latter she converted to Buddhism and was willing to let bygones be bygones and give the groom a second chance when she reencountered him in Wales, which happily culminated April 1 when they took their vows before an audience that included 32 baaing sheep, 14 bleating goats, two ornery yaks and a spitting camel.

Dr. Mendoza-Frack (as she will be known professionally), 34, has a bachelor's degree in pyrotechnics from Combustible Technical College in Bogota, Columbia, a master's degrees in sparkle and glitter from The Fashion Institute of Glitz in Twinkle, Texas and doctoral degree in genital science from Oxford University. At the present time she is employed by the Federal Bureau of Investigation in Atlanta as an undescended testicle detector for the Southeastern United States. She is also an Arctic Circle certified snowflake and icicle collector and owns the largest collection of snowflakes and icicles in the Western Hemisphere.

The bride is the daughter of Myra Gonzalez Mendoza and Humberto Mendoza of Medellin, Columbia. Her mother, who is afflicted with a chronic case of pink eye, is a bobsled instructor and captain of the Columbia national bobsled team. She has twice represented Columbia in the winter Olympics as a bobsledder, and has also represented her country in the summer Olympics in horseshoe tossing. The father of the bride owns a company that manufactures cherry bombs and Roman candles. He is a former mohel who between 1972 and 1996 circumcised more than 10,000 babies in South America. In 1997 he was forced to retire after a medical condition (specifically, essential tremor, a neurological disease that causes rhythmic and involuntary shaking of the hands) was responsible for an unfortunate accident at a bris.

The bride's paternal great grandfather Simon Bolivar Mendoza, who was a cross dresser and pen pal of Helen Keller, was the Vice President of Columbia from 1943 to 1953. He was also the Chinese checkers champion of South America for 44 years.

The groom, 36, is a high school dropout who served eight years in the United States Marine corps where he attained the rank of lance corporal. Although he was acquitted in 2002 by a military court of charges related to arson and lewd behavior, he was dishonorably discharged from the corps in 2003 for urinating on a superior officer's shoes. Between 2003 and 2011 Mr. Frack worked as a part-time chimney sweeper, mime and National Football League referee. In 2012 he traveled to England to be treated for a nasty toe fungus and to study topiary. After being arrested in Oxford in 2012 for public indecency he was incarcerated for 16 months. While in prison he successfully completed two 12 step treatment programs for sexual disinhibition and urinary incontinence. Upon his release he settled in Cardiff, Wales where he has become an acclaimed topiary artist, specializing in sculpting phantasmagorical mythical creatures and male genitalia from trees and shrubs. In his spare time Mr. Frack, who recently converted to Buddhism, is a volunteer counselor at Rotting Digits, a support service for sufferers of toe fungus and parasitic diseases of the extremities.

The groom is the son of Philomena Frack of Alcatraz Island, California. Ms. Frack, who describes herself as a "proud militant illiterate," is a professional fossil hunter who also works six months a year in Las Vegas as a Cher impersonator. Although neither the groom nor his mother know the identity of his biological father, later this year the two of them are scheduled to appear on the syndicated American television show "Maury" where multiple DNA tests conducted on three different men may finally reveal his paternity.

# Predestination and Ivan Hoe

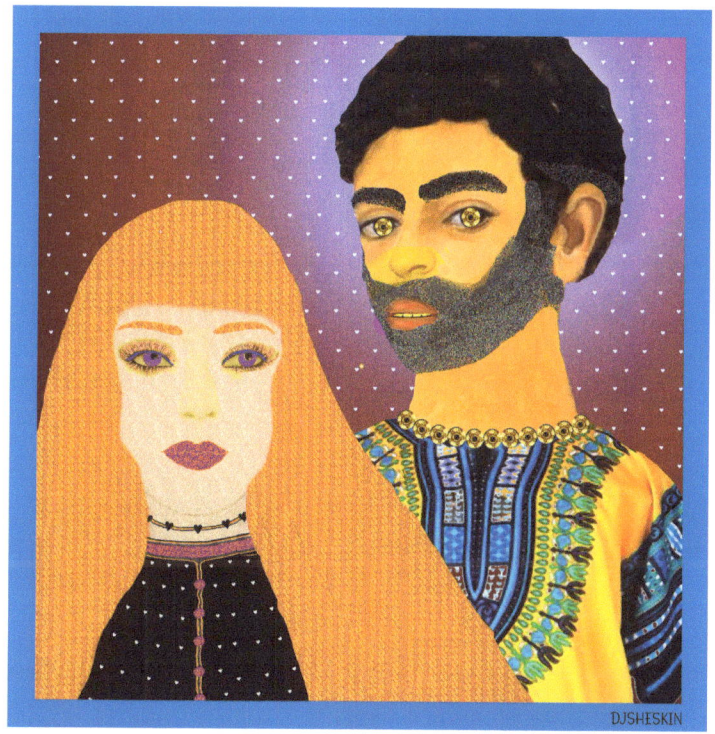

The singer-songwriter Predestination (who was born Deana Rho Mineeka) and Nobel Laureate Ivan Hoe were married April 11 in Stockholm, Sweden. Premonition, the bride's identical twin sister, who was authorized to serve as a conjugal priestess for the day by the European Union Marriage Ministries, officiated with the aid of Albedo Flash, a visiting secular agnostic priest from Uruguay. An ultra-denominational ceremony followed by a lavish banquet was held at the Stockholm Concert Hall. Among the notables in attendance were King Carl XVI Gustaf of Sweden, King Harald V of Norway, Faure Gnassingbè (the President of Togo) and supermodel Cicely Skin, who is the bride's former nanny and current world record holder for consuming the most Jell-O in twenty-four hours.

According to the bride, the couple first met in northern Maine on May 14, 2013 when while hiking through the woods looking for four leaf clovers she came upon a bearded giant who greeted her in a dialect that she surmised to be some mixture of French, Croatian and Russian. Instead of being frightened, Predestination, who is multilingual, found him compelling and the two of them returned to her vacation cabin. That evening the man confided to her his unique history compounded by the fact that he had no name. The next morning as the couple went into the woods to forage for mushrooms and legumes, a dwarf riding atop a unicorn emerged from a cluster of beech trees and declared that the two of them were destined to spend the rest of their lives together and from that point forward the man should be known as Ivan Hoe.

The bride, 33, is a world renowned singer and songwriter whose record sales, according to the Record Industry Association of America, exceed 80 million. Her latest number one album "Hybrid Hens" is her 16th platinum record. She is also an acclaimed actress who will be appearing this summer at the Public Shakespeare Theater in New York's Central Park in the role of Peppercorn in the premier of "The Libra Who Loved Szechwan Food." In 2015 she won a Tony Award for her role as Dandelion in Tennessee Williams recently discovered play "The Passion of Naomi Wilderness," and won an Academy Award in 2016 for best actress as the bipolar dressmaker Dreidel in the Steven Spielberg movie "Chutzpa,"

The bride is the daughter of Mimi Aries Mineeka and Dr. Vincent Mineeka of Berkeley, California. Her father is an orthomolecular psychiatrist who has a private practice in Berkeley. He is also seer and eighth generation ancestor on his mother's side of the French physician and renowned prophet Nostradamus. The bride's mother has been a crop circle designer for the past 47 years, in spite of the fact that during much of that time she has been confined to a wheelchair as a result of injuries she sustained in 1982 when a large ball of twine on display on the lawn of the Sacramento Museum of Unconventional Art rolled down a hill and collided with a bicycle she was riding.

The groom, 41, who is seven feet tall, was a hermit for 29 years. As noted earlier, he emerged from the woods of northern Maine on May 14, 2013. During his more than a quarter century of isolation he self-schooled himself in numerous subjects including quantum physics, linguistics, medical genetics, hematology, endocrinology, embryology, organic and inorganic chemistry, invertebrate and vertebrate zoology, ornithology, herpetology, plant physiology, knot theory, algebraic topology, combinatorics, Boolean algebra, Fourier analysis, game theory, number theory, fluid mechanics, and French cooking. He is fluent in 12 languages and able to play14 musical instruments. In spite of the fact that there is no record of him ever graduating from high school, in 2014 Mr. Hoe was appointed to the endowed Albert Einstein Chair of Higher Mathematics and Theoretical Physics at the Massachusetts Institute of Technology. Since 2014 Mr. Hoe has had 38 papers published in peer reviewed journals, and is the first person to be awarded the Fields medal in mathematics twice (2015 and 2016) for solving the Hodge conjecture, a previously unsolved problem in the field of algebraic geometry, and Barnette's conjecture, a previously unsolved problem in graph theory. In 2018 he became the only person to win both the Fields medal and a Nobel Prize when he was awarded the Nobel Prize in physics for his work on the relationship between antimatter and rainbows.

According to Mr. Hoe, like Moses, he was abandoned at birth by his biological parents. He has little or no recollection of who may have adopted him and for how long he was kept. All he claims to remember is that at the age of 12 he fled into the woods of northern Maine where he learned to survive and remained until 2013. During his time in the woods he had numerous visions that bequeathed to him the knowledge he required to survive and to master all of the subjects in which he has become fluent. He states that in the middle of the night on May 13, 2013 he was awakened from a deep sleep by a brilliant sphere of light from which emerged an amorphous entity who told him it was time for him to become a citizen of the world and to pass on his wealth of knowledge to the human race.

# Gertrude Alon and Olaf Orojel

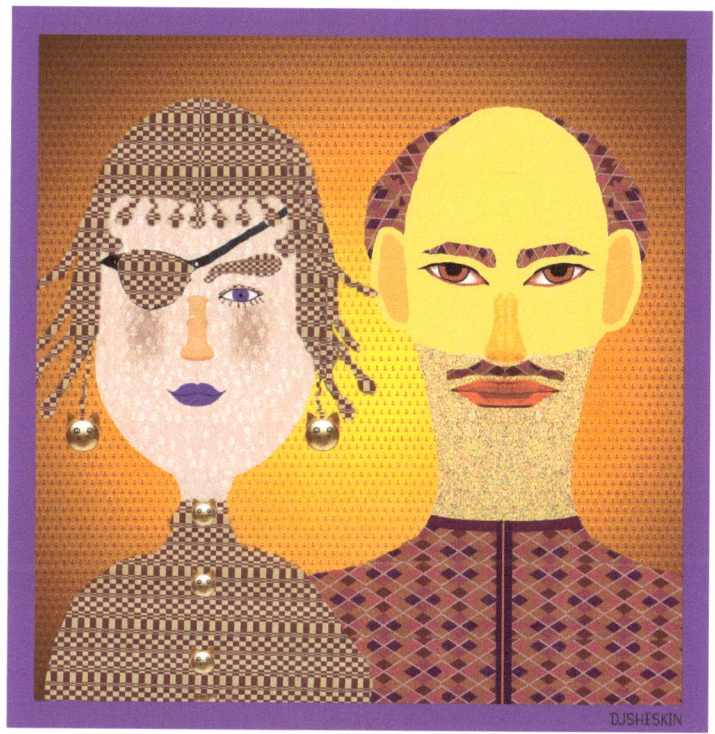

**G**ertrude Alon and Olaf Orojel were married May 19 in Derry, New Hampshire by television personality and recipient of the first face transplant in New England, Chu-Chu Cho, who was ordained for four hours as a Northern New England Life and Death minister for occasional weddings and funerals.

Ms. Alon, 36, who has a wooden leg and wears a patch over her right eye, is a professional tap dancer affiliated with Tap of the Line, the preeminent tap dancing school in Northern New England. She is a graduate of The Nijinsky Academy of Dance and Culture in Moscow, Idaho with specialties in Mambo and Rhumba and a subspecialty in Bolero. Although the bride is a self-taught tap dancer, she is recognized by both the World Tap Dancing Institute and The American Tap Dancing Foundation as a Level 5 Master, the highest rating awarded in the craft. Ms. Alon is an avid collector of air sickness bags and a passionate advocate of people who have received face transplants.

The bride is the daughter of Mimi Alon and Dr. Vincent Alon of Avon, Connecticut. The bride's father is a professor of suppository science at the Connecticut School of Proctology, and is considered the world's leading expert on the treatment of anal fissures. He is also the founder of CryoPet, the only organization in New England devoted to cryogenically freezing household pets for future resuscitation. The bride's mother has been a successful dominatrix for the past 27 years, in spite of the fact that during that time she has been suffering from an antifungal resistant yeast infection. Like her daughter, she too is a collector — in her case, she hoards used condoms and discarded antidepressant prescriptions.

The groom, 39, is a graduate of Hook, Line and Sinker School of Angling in Spoiled Bait, Wyoming where he is presently employed as an instructor in the department of fish tails and canoe science. Among the courses he teaches are ice fishing, fly fishing, chumming, fish gutting and water bailing. He is the author of the best-selling books "Copulating in a Canoe without Capsizing" (Lubricated Prophylactic Press, 2010) and "Piranha Confidential" (Fishbone Books, 2013). For the past 23 years Mr. Orojel has supplemented his income by serving as a professional sperm donor. His ejaculate is so highly sought after by sperm banks that it commands a price of $1500 or more per ounce.

The groom is the son of Thora and Orville Orojel of Toronto, Canada. His mother, who last month was put in in a medically induced coma as a result of suffering from hiccups for 645 consecutive days, is currently on leave from her job as director of the Benito Mussolini Foundation, an organization devoted to rehabilitating the image of the late Italian fascist dictator. The groom's father is a commodities trader with the Toronto Mercantile Exchange whose specialty is trading sugar and spice and everything nice. During periods of financial downswings the groom's father rents beach umbrellas and wet suits to vacationing diplomats on the shores of Lake Ontario.

The couple met at the wedding of the groom's sister and husband Umberto Mussolini, who is the great grandson of Benito Mussolini. On their first date Ms. Alon and Mr. Orojel went fishing on Captain Barney's Spanish Galleon, a Lake Ontario fishing charter boat, where the groom caught what is thought to be a world record 51 pound rainbow trout. The couple shared their first kiss two weeks later in the middle of Lake Erie in a thunderstorm while bailing out a kayak they had rented that had become flooded with rainwater.

# Patricia Pocahontas Goldberg and Chief Evening Storm

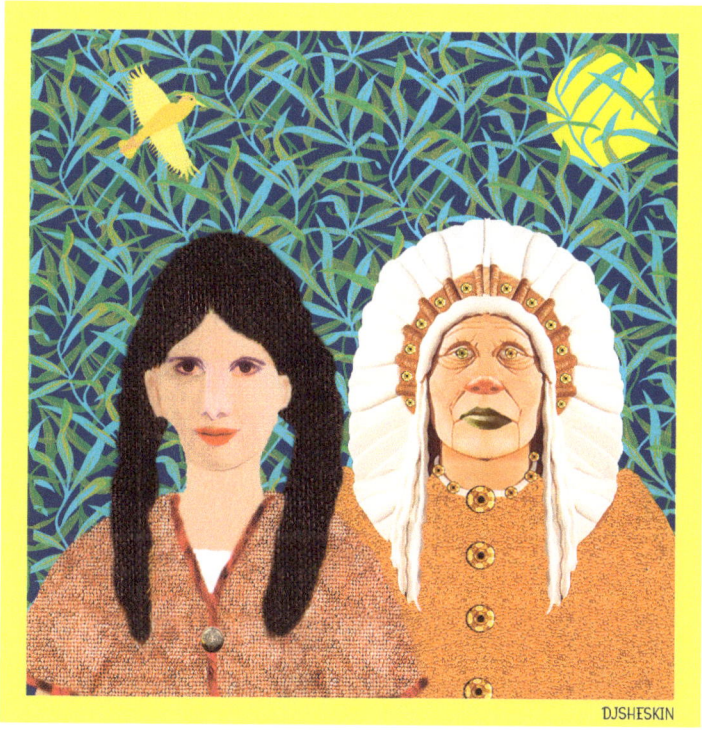

DJSHESKIN

**P**atricia Pocahontas Goldberg and Chief Evening Storm were married May 31 in a large teepee situated on the shores of the Great Salt Lake in Utah. With the aid of the Native American medicine man Orange Fox, who perfused the air with scents of the sacred plants peyote, cannabis, sage, cedar and sweetgrass, a cosmic universal ceremony was performed in Yiddish by Rabbi Geronimo Schwartz, who was designated for the day as an Honorary Elder of the Oklevueha Native American Church by the Chief of The Seven Tribal Nations.

The bride, 18, who is wise beyond her years, was a child prodigy who graduated from kindergarten at the age of 1, grade school at the age of 3, middle school at the age of 5, high school at the age of 7, and at the age of 10 received a bachelor of arts degree, magna cum laude, in rhetoric and folklore from Shakespeare University in Stratford-upon-Avon, England. In 2012 she was awarded a Ph.D. in limericks and sonnets from Elizabeth Barret Browning University in Edinburgh, Scotland, and is currently doing postdoctoral work at the Institute of Haiku and Gnomic Verse in Dublin, Ireland where she is conducting research on garden gnomes and leprechauns.

The bride is the daughter of Dr. Penny Schwartz Goldberg and the late Harvey Goldberg of New York City. The bride's mother is a board certified cosmetic surgeon who specializes in navel puckering, vulva sculpting and testicle enlargement. She is also a docent and outreach educator at The Museum of Foreskins and Placentas in Newark, New Jersey. The bride's late father, who is the only known person in the world to have died from geographic tongue, was a partner in the law firm Wynken, Blynken and Nod, where he specialized in nursery rhyme law. The bride is the stepdaughter of Milton Goldberg, the younger brother of her late father, who is President of the American Association for Nude Recreation, the leading organization in the United States that advocates for nudity.

The groom, 53, is a Chief on the Kaibab Paiute reservation in Arizona 50 miles north of the Grand Canyon. He is a graduate of Navaho Christian University where he majored in animistic theology and minored in wilderness literature. For the past five years he has been an editorial writer for the Grand Canyon Times where he has a weekly column entitled "Pumpkins, Peyote and Polytheism."

The groom is the son of the late Sacheen Shining Blossom and Dark Descending Sky, a revered Paiute Elder who died from a scorpion sting in 2015. The groom's mother was a naturopathic healer whose specialty was employing herbs such as chamomile, ginkgo and ginger in the treatment of sunburn, windburn and heartburn. His father was a sheep shearer and shaman who served as a consultant to DreamWorks Pictures on matters relating to Native American folklore and powwow protocol.

The couple met in 2014 through the dating website Jane Austen Meets Sitting Bull.

# Pebble Song and Zachary Bolte

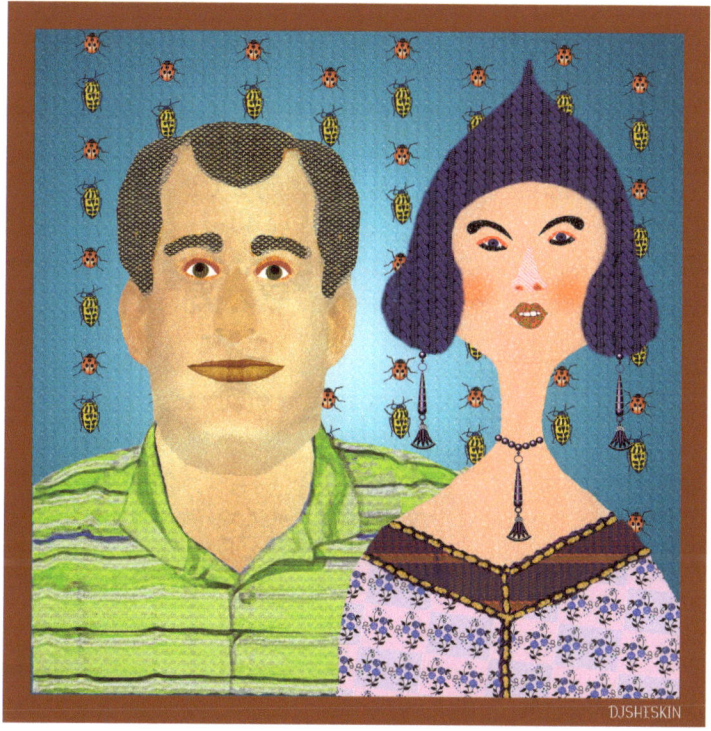

**P**ebble Song and Zachary Bolte were married June 6 on the Great Wall of China in Zhangjiakou (which is 164 kilometers northwest of Beijing). A joint ceremony was conducted in Mandarin by Taoist Celestial Master Sungyuou Pou, and in Cajun English by the atheist redneck metaphysician Emmanuel Bolte. The latter Mr. Bolte is a half-brother of the groom and former boyfriend of the bride who stalked Ms. Song for six months until she was forced to get a restraining order on him that expired one week before the wedding. The couple was blessed in front of seven family members, eight pilgrims who happened to be walking the wall in search of lost or discarded jewelry and nine packhorses that bore on their backs gifts from North America and smuggled contraband from Eastern Europe.

The bride, 24, graduated magna cum laude from Madame Mao University in Beijing with a teaching certificate in the visual and culinary arts. She has a master's degree from Bamboo Agricultural Institute in plowing and irrigation. Ms. Song is currently employed by the People's Aesthetic

Agrarian Cooperative where she teaches primary and middle school students how to integrate rice, barley and soybeans into Sichuan casseroles and mixed media works of art.

The bride is the daughter of Heidi Song and Mao Song of San Francisco, California. The bride's mother, who was born in Switzerland to bipolar parents, is a professional yodeler who in addition to teaching yodeling teaches courses in sipping, burping, belching, sucking and gargling at the Institute of Oral and Aural Arts in San Francisco. She is an award winning songwriter who wrote the 2006 Grammy award winning song "Salt Water Purge," which is said to have inspired the cult movie "Gargle Girls." Ms. Song's father is an aquatics guru at Bay Area Aquamarine where he teaches quadriplegics to swim and dolphins to play water polo.

The groom, 35, has a bachelor's degree in fine arts from Da Vinci University in Florence, South Carolina, and a doctoral degree in art restoration from the University of Rome in Rome, Georgia. For the past two years he has been a visiting art restorer at the Chairman Mao Museum of Rehabilitated Art in Shanghai, China, where he oversees the restoration of paintings that were damaged by the Japanese during their occupation of China in the 1930s. The groom also studied Polynesian crafts at The Institute of Tiki Culture on Easter Island, and for the past five years has run workshops in Oceania and East Asia on toothpick art and drink umbrella design. Mr. Bolte is a recovering glue sniffing addict who takes pride in the fact that he not sniffed an inhalant for18 years.

The groom is the son of Adelaide LeRoux Bolte of Lafayette, Louisiana and the late Barney Bolte. His mother is a third generation perfumer and the owner and president of Adelaide's Aromas LLC, an international manufacturer of fragrances and scented candles. The groom's father was a genetic engineer who sold four headed roosters and two headed sheep to carnivals before his business was shut down in 1999 by the Department of Animal Husbandry, Dairying and Fisheries. He died in 2003 as a result of an inhalant overdose while he was working as an intern testing aromatic hydrocarbons in the research division of Adelaide's Aromas.

The couple met in 2011 on the United States island territory Guam when Mr. Bolte hired Ms. Song as a teaching assistant in his popular Polynesian craft workshop "Psychedelic Drink Umbrellas for Cocktails and Highballs."

# Puja Virenda Parikh and Jamison Lafitte

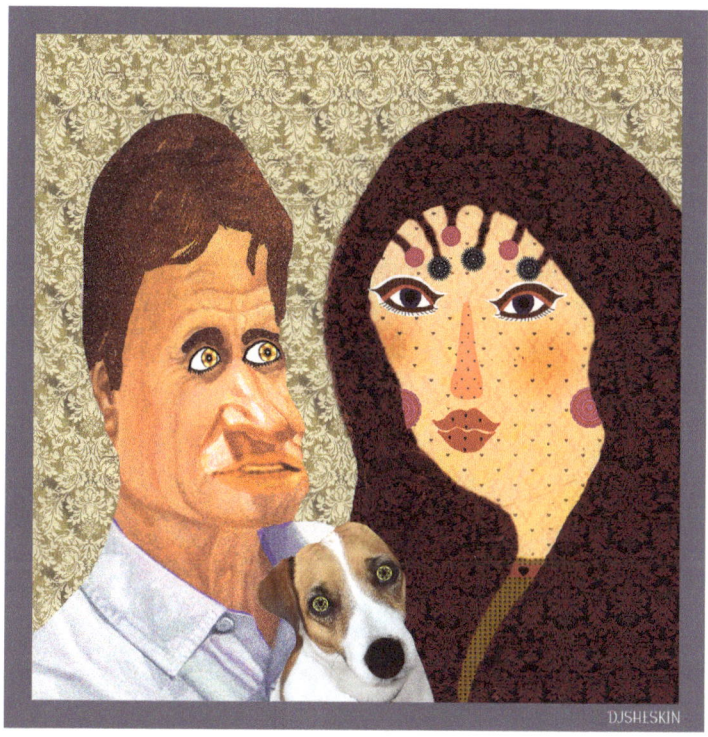

**P**uja Virenda Parikh and Jamison Lafitte were married June 19 in Lake Charles, Louisiana. The ceremony took place at the Pelican House, a country manor overlooking a swamp populated with alligators and other bayou wildlife. Pastor Roudanez Andre, a Creole minister, officiated the event aided by Pandit Dharma Prabhakar, a Hindu priest, who added elements from the Vedas to the couple's vows. The ceremony was televised throughout Louisiana and videotaped for further viewing on Louisiana Public Television.

The couple met at the 2013 U.S. Open Tennis Championships at the USTA National Tennis Center in Flushing Meadows, Queens where Ms. Parikh and Mr. Lafitte were competing against one another in a mixed doubles match. After the match, which Ms. Parikh and her partner, (who at the time was her finance) won, Mr. Lafitte was so smitten that he followed her half-way around the world for a year and a half to finally win her hand when she accepted his proposal following her loss during the mixed doubles quarterfinals at 2015 French Open Championships in Paris.

The bride, 29, has a master of science degree from the New Delhi Institute of Horticulture where she majored in hydroponics (the cultivation of flowers, fruits and vegetables without the use of soil). She is currently the arboretum director at Floral Heaven in Sulfur Springs, Louisiana. Ms. Parikh is the only person in the world known to grow Venus flytraps, a carnivorous plant, hydroponically. She is also the only person known to sell Venus Flytraps as a chemical-free environmentally friendly method of pest control. Ms. Parikh is a former member of the Indian National Tennis Association who represented India in Davis Cup competition for eight years. During her career as a professional tennis player she won 26 national or international titles in doubles and mixed doubles events.

The bride is the daughter of Padma and Karam Parikh of Mumbai. Her mother is a former phlebotomist who for the past 15 years has been the director of the Mumbai Blood Bank. In 2006 she was prosecuted and convicted by the Indian state of Maharashtra for accepting the blood of members of the Untouchable caste for transfusion into members of higher castes. After a three year legal battle her conviction was overturned by the Indian Supreme Court, which declared that blood banks could collect Untouchable blood for general distribution. The bride's father is a rug weaver whose hand-weaved wool, silk and cotton rugs are considered among the finest in the world. At a recent auction in London one of his wool rugs sold for $125,000. On a darker note, in 2014 the body of the Indian politician Kishor Charhury, who had been abducted by terrorists in 2013, was found at the bottom of the Chambal River in Central India wrapped in one of Parikh's rugs.

The groom, 34, who because of his unusually long nose goes by the nickname of Pinocchio, is a snuff tester in the Lake Charles office of Philip Morris International, one of the world's largest producers of tobacco products. He is a graduate of Lake Charles high school where in 2001 he was Louisiana Quarterback of the Year. He attended Louisiana State University for two years on a football scholarship where he was a member of both the varsity football and tennis teams. He left college in 2004 to pursue a career as professional tennis player which ended abruptly when a disoriented seagull flew into his face during a tennis match in Florida, causing extensive damage to his right eye and already misshapen nose.

The groom is the son of Delphine Lafitte of Baton Rouge and the late

Edwige Lafitte. The groom's mother, who has had multiple rhinoplasties for a deviated septum as well as for cosmetic reasons, is the current secretary of the Pinocchio Society, an organization dedicated to the support of people with long or misshapen noses. His father, an inveterate user of chewing tobacco who succumbed to oral cancer in 1994, was the health and lifestyle editor for the Times-Picayune of New Orleans for 23 years.

Mr. Lafitte and Ms. Parikh will share their new home with a recently rescued Jack Russell terrier they have named Geppetto.

# Ellen Tubbs and Hami Okajabe

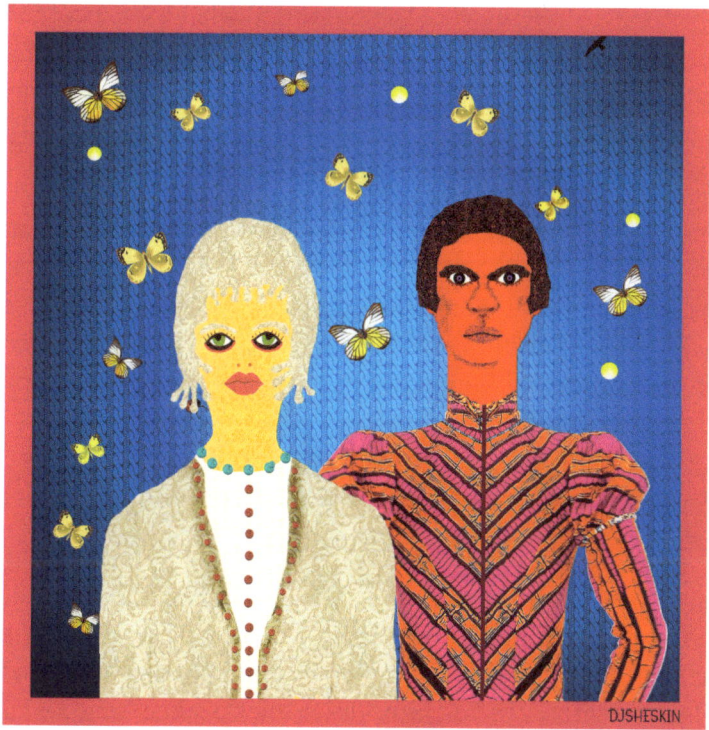

Ellen Tubbs and Hami Okajabe were married June 26 at Lake Mburo National Park in Uganda. The ceremony was performed in Swahili by the Bantu witch doctor and exorcist Vanyaunyau, with the Wiccan priestess Iris Venon adding elements in Old English to the couple's vows. The wedding was catered by Kaikara Amin, the great granddaughter of the late Ugandan dictator Idi Amin.

The bride, 32, who is a practitioner of Wicca, has a bachelor of arts degree in tabloid journalism from the Ann Landers and Abigail Van Buren School of Journalism at Atheist Christian University in Confessor, Texas. She is a nationally syndicated advice columnist who also has a weekly television show on the FOX network in which she dispenses advice to aspiring debutantes on issues relating to pubic lice and fried rice. She is the author of the best-selling books "Hookup or Fookup" (Promiscuous Press, 2014) and "Let's Get It On" (Wonton Books, 2016). Ms. Tubbs is a 128 time nose bleed survivor.

The bride is the daughter of Myra Kelp Tubbs of Dallas, Texas and the late Teddy "Tubby" Tubbs. The bride's father, who at one point in his life weighed over 500 pounds, was an architect who gained notoriety in 2002 when a 56 story skyscraper he designed collapsed resulting in death of 2345 people. The following year he committed what some people consider to be a heroic and symbolic suicide by leaping out of an airplane without a parachute onto the condemned site of his collapsed skyscraper. The bride's mother is doily designer and works part time as the only topless exterminator in the Southwestern United States.

The groom, 44, has a bachelor's degree in counterfeiting from Ndejje University in Kampala, Uganda and a master's degree in arbitrage from The London School of Finance in London, England. He is an itinerant peddler who sells everything and anything from bottle caps to vintage jewelry in the streets of Kampala off a wooden cart pulled by a horse. Although the groom still has a full head of hair, during the past five years he has become an avid collector of toupees and brimless caps (such as kufis and yarmulkes) which he attributes to his fear of dying from male pattern baldness.

The groom is the son of Namono Okajabe of Kamapala and the late Sanyu Okajabe. The groom's mother is a former debutante who was introduced in 1973 at a ball in Nairobi, Kenya. She is a bail bondswoman and bounty hunter who specializes in tracking down pickpockets and serial killers. The groom's father was an acclaimed author of books on slugs and snails until he was accused of plagiarism by the prominent Ugandan witch doctor Joseph Mugoya. He died in 2006 from an infection caused by a roundworm that had invaded his central nervous system as a result of him eating a Great African land snail on a dare from one of his five wives while the two of them were parasailing over Victoria Falls in Zambia.

The groom's grandfather Asal Okajabe, who was a fierce advocate for "little people," claimed responsibility for starting a fire that burned 300,000 acres in the Bwindi Impenetrable National Park in Uganda as a way of protesting the government's shoddy treatment of pygmies.

The couple, who met at a concert in Kampala that celebrated the life of the late and infamous Ugandan dictator Idi Amin, plan to establish homes in both Dallas and Kampala.

# Iris Tannenbaum and Michel Parks

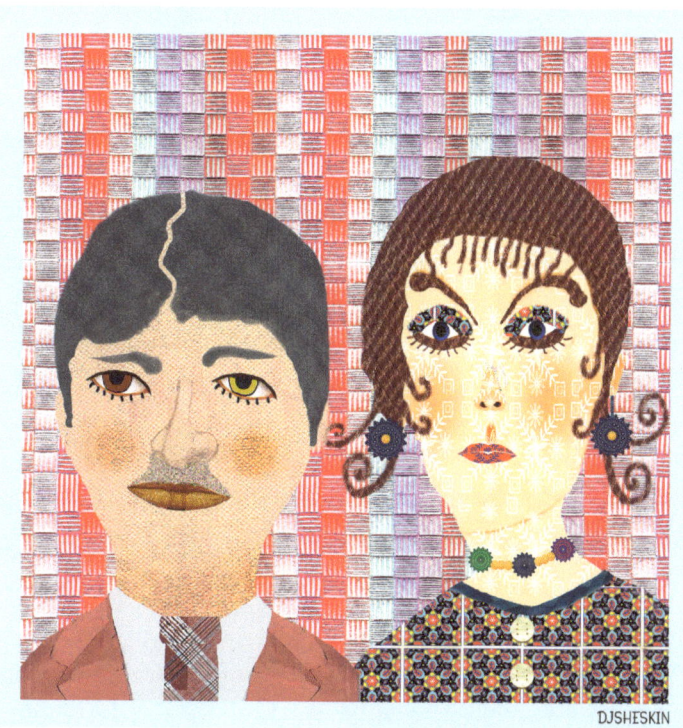

DJSHESKIN

Wearing a distressed denim organic cotton bridal gown made by members of the Untouchable caste in India, a soy silk veil made by Buddhist monks in Tibet and industrial hemp shoes made by abused women in Refuge House, a women's shelter in downtown Los Angeles, on June 30 Iris Nadine Tannenbaum was married to Michel Parks who was wearing an optic yellow Ralph Lauren wetsuit, The ceremony, which took place 250 miles southwest of San Diego on the Carnival Cruise Line ship Neptune's Fury, was officiated by the vessel's captain Thorson Borgland, who was aided by the bride's yellow-napped amazon parrot Banana who inserted avian elements into the couple's vows.

The bride and groom met serendipitously in 2016 on a Royal Caribbean cruise to St. Martin when they were forced to abandon their ship which had been attacked by terrorists, and found themselves alone in a life boat stranded in the middle of the Atlantic Ocean.

The bride, 29, has an associate of fine arts degree in belts and bandanas from

The Haute Couture Institute in the Republic of Georgia. Because she has multiple environmental sensitivities, including severe allergies to velvet, leather and cashmere, Ms. Tannenbaum has become a vocal proponent of organic, ecologically friendly apparel. Since 2014 she has owned and operated Iris Eyes Are Smiling, an appointment-only boutique in Beverly Hills where she sells assorted curios such as seahorse saddles, unicorn horns, leopard spots and tiger stripes to a select clientele of celebrities and diplomats who are not permitted to wear perfume, deodorant or any type of scented product in her presence. The bride donates 25% of all her boutique's profits to Afloat and Well, an organization that supports former cruise ship passengers who have survived terrorist attacks and norovirus outbreaks.

The bride is the daughter of Lily and Micah Tannenbaum of Los Angeles. The bride's mother is a life-long trichotillomaniac who sells human hair to companies that manufacture tresses and wigs. Her father is a professional videographer whose specialty is videotaping autopsies and cremations. He is also a poet who has most recently published the best-selling collection of bawdy limericks "There Was a Young Man" (Prurient Press, 2017).

The groom, 37, is a graduate of the Julliard School of Music and was the Gold Medalist at the 2008 Van Cliburn International Piano Competition. He plays the piano weeknights at O'Shaughnessy's Bar in downtown Los Angeles, and on weekends collaborates with two down on their luck former Van Cliburn winners to provide entertainment at bar mitzvahs and orgies.

The groom is the son of Dr. Marsha Parks of Los Angeles and Orville Parks of Memphis, Tennessee. His mother is a board certified neurosurgeon whose specialty is performing lobotomies on vanquished dictators and defrocked clergy. She is also a part-time bouncer at O'Shaughnessy's Bar. Mr. Park's father, who is a high functioning alcoholic, is an alchemist who has transformed sand, silt and gravel into gold, and has recently discovered a way to convert human dandruff into uranium.

# Wilhelmina Amsberg ter Reif and Abdullah bin Saud

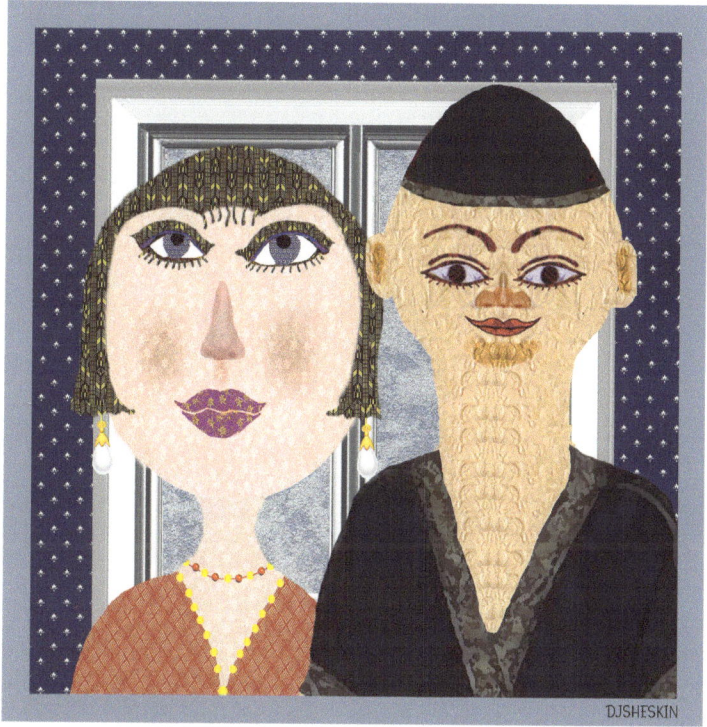

DJSHESKIN

**W**ilhelmina Amsberg ter Reif and Abdullah bin Saud were married July3 in a Walmart parking lot in Tullytown, Pennsylvania in an impromptu ceremony officiated by Bucks County Justice of the Peace Eddie Sparks. The only other parties present for the event were the bride's emotional support dog Caspar, who drooled throughout the ceremony, and the groom's three other wives, all of whom spat at the bride when she said "I do."

The bride, 31, claims she is a former Crown Princess of the Holland who abdicated her right to the throne in 2005 when she emancipated herself from the Dutch royal family to pursue a career as a topless waitress. Ms. ter Reif, whose three previous marriages ended in divorce, contends that she has a bachelor's degree in pet sitting from Erasmus University and a master of fine arts degree in facial peeling from The Dutch Institute of Luminous Skin. Prior to marrying Mr. bin Saud the bride worked intermittently as a bowtie designer, an erotic sports memorabilia telemarketer and as a topless dog groomer.

Ms. ter Reif alleges she is the daughter of the late Claus von Amsberg and Juliana piet Loo, the former King and Queen of Holland. Her father is best remembered for a clandestine fifteen year love affair he had with a dyslexic German linguist who tutored all of his children. The bride's mother, who was a podiatry school dropout, was a passionate advocate of foot care who raised consciousness in Europe regarding the dangers associated with untreated corns and bunions.

Mr. bin Saud, 38, claims to be a member of the Saudi royal family and that he is twelfth in line to ascend to the throne. He states that he has a bachelor's degree in camouflage and duplicity from the University of Riyadh and a master's degree in fine art forgery from Oxford University. He is a freelance extortionist and bigamist who delights in pulling off scams and grifts.

The groom maintains that he is the 25th son of King Salman bin Abdulaziz Al Saud and his eighth wife Fahda. The groom's father is best known for advocating polygamy and beheading. The groom can provide few details about his mother since she, along with his father's 34 other wives, is sequestered in a palace closely guarded by an army of eunuchs and elves.

The couple met earlier this year in a Walmart parking lot in Parsippany, New Jersey when Ms. ter Reif observed Mr. bin Saud siphoning gasoline from a vintage 1956 Cadillac De Ville coupe. When she promised not to alert the authorities if he bought her a drink, the groom, captivated by her blond hair and blue eyes, obliged and subsequently initiated her into a life of crime and grime.

After a two month honeymoon to a location that is nobody's business the couple plans to be homeless.

# Cookie Goose and Malcom Charming

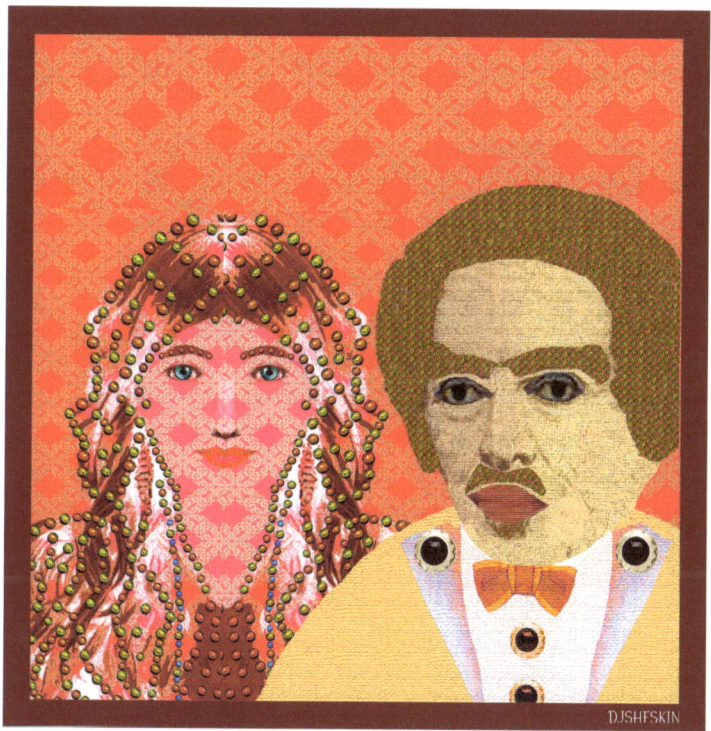

Cookie Goose and Malcolm Charming were married July 26 at The Magic Kingdom in Bay Lake, Florida. The wedding, which was held on the Prince Charming Regal Carousel, was officiated by Gary Darling, a Milky Way Life oracle, who was aided by the bride's mother, Minna Goose, who periodically inserted clichés derived from fairy tales and nursery rhymes into the couple's vows.

The bride, 30, has a bachelor's degree from Hans Christian Anderson University in Odense, Denmark where she majored in hallucinations and delusions. For the past three years she has been employed in Las Vegas, Nevada as a blackjack dealer for Dreams Come True, a for-profit organization that encourages gambling among people with addictive personalities. Prior that that she worked as a cadaver dog trainer for the state of Nevada.

The bride is the daughter of Minna and Cable Goose of Old MacDonald, Arkansas. The bride's mother, who has a bachelor's degree in nursery rhymes from The Jack and Jill Institute of Frolic and a doctoral degree in fairy tales from Rumpelstiltskin University, is the owner of Absolute Karma, a company that markets good luck charms such as rabbit's feet and four leaf clovers to people who have never won the lottery. She is also the author of two controversial best-selling books, "Little Red Riding Hood Was Six Feet Tall and Weighed Over 300 Pounds" (Grimm Brothers Press, 1997) and "Little Bo Peep Was Anorexic" (Three Blind Mice, 2002). The bride's father, who is retired, was employed for 40 years by Ringling Brothers and Barnum and Bailey where he variously worked as ringmaster, a sword swallower and, on occasion, masqueraded as the bearded lady.

The groom, 42, who Ms. Goose lovingly refers to as "My Prince Charming," has been an imaginary friend of the bride for the past 25 years. As for his education and credentials, on any given day he is whatever Ms. Goose imagines him to be. Since the groom is little more than a figment of her imagination, if he has parents then no doubt they will view her as the daughter-in-law they always wanted.

Insofar as Ms. Goose can remember, her first encounter with the groom was when she was seven years old and he materialized out of thin air as she was awakening from a deep sleep the morning after her beloved basset hound and best friend Mr. Puggles died. From that day forward Mr. Charming has been there to support her and help her through hard times.

# Moira Keys and Sheldon Goldstein

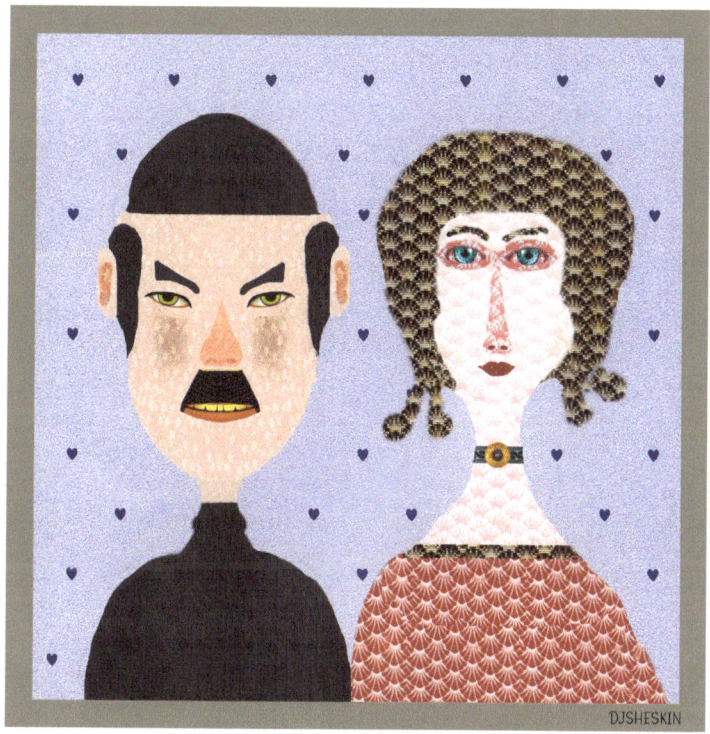

Along with 986 other couples, Moira Keys and Sheldon Goldstein were married July 30 in Madison Square Garden as part of a mass ceremony officiated by the Reverend Hyung Jin Moon. The bride and groom's marriage was prearranged by the Reverend Moon, who is a third generation relative of the late Reverend Sun Myung Moon, the founder of the Unification Church in 1954.

The couple, both of whom had become disillusioned with their religious heritages, met for the first time fifteen minutes before the marriage ceremony.

The bride, 28, is a magna cum laude graduate of Purification University in Inferno, Spain where she majored in exorcisms and played four years of varsity rugby. Up until last month she was employed as an exorcist by the Catholic diocese of New York, and at the present time is the only accredited female exorcist in North America. Ms. Keys, who has an unsightly birthmark on her left cheek that is the exact shape of Argentina, candidly admits that for the past five years she has been desperate to get married, and previously applied to but had not been selected to be a participant on the television show "Married at First Sight," in which multiple couples matched by experts get married upon seeing one another for the first time.

The bride is the daughter of Penelope Keys of Buffalo, New York and Brady Locks Keys of Cape Breton Island, Nova Scotia. The bride's mother is employed by the American Academy of Dentistry as a counselor for people who have untreatable halitosis. Ms. Keys's father has been a seasonal lighthouse keeper off the coast of Nova Scotia for 16 years. He is a professional log roller who regularly participates in competitions in the Eastern Canadian provinces and Northern New England. He is also an accomplished musician who has been contracted by Sony Music to record all of Mozart's symphonies playing an accordion.

The groom, 30, who has Tourette's disorder, is the son of Zalmar Goldstein, Grand Rebe of the Satmar Hassidim congregation in New City, New York. After completing his Orthodox Jewish education at Yeshiva Ruach Chaim in Williamsburg, Brooklyn, Mr. Goldstein graduated from Yeshiva University of Mining and Agriculture in Matzo Ball, Montana with a bachelor's degree in rhetorical chutzpah. Although his lifelong dream was to be an emcee at mineral and vegetable shows, because of his Tourette's condition he has been forced to maintain a lower profile and be the person behind the scenes who washes and shines the merchandise.

The groom is the son of Zalmar and Myra Goldstein of New City, New York. In addition to being the Grand Rebe of Satmar Hassidim, the groom's father, who also has Tourette's disorder, regularly travels around the country to encourage individuals with mental and behavioral challenges to become members of the clergy. The groom's mother, who is the daughter of the late Grand Rebe Ishmail Cohn of Jerusalem, makes booties and vests for domestic pets to wear in inclement weather.

The couple have made a commitment to raise money for the Unification Church for one year. After that they have agreed that they will both return to school to study either potato farming or urban legends.

# Aroma Rose and Saffron Peppercorn

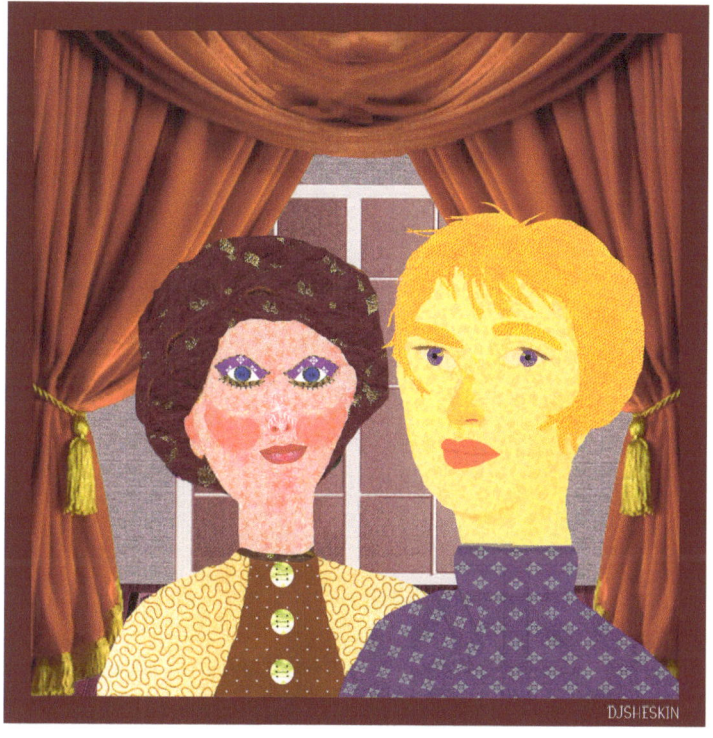

Aroma Rose and Saffron Peppercorn were married August 4 in the Northern Lights chapel at the Aurora Borealis Hotel in Juneau, Alaska. The ceremony was jointly officiated by Mellow Amber, one of Ms. Rose's former girlfriends, and Samuel "Salty" O'Malley, a former boyfriend of Ms. Peppercorn, both of whom were appointed as civil celebrants for the event.

The couple met in 2014 in Yumen, China during a bubonic plague outbreak when Ms. Peppercorn contracted the disease and Ms. Rose, who was quarantined in the same building, helped nurse her back to health.

In 2010 Ms. Rose, 31, was declared dead shortly after she went into a coma as a result of liver failure resulting from years of drug and alcohol abuse. However, after being injected with an experimental drug she was miraculously revived and shortly thereafter was the successful recipient of a liver transplant. Since graduating from the renowned drug treatment program Molecule Free in Port Hollis, Maine, Ms. Rose has obtained a bachelor's degree in beekeeping from Intuit University in Umiat, Alaska and a master's degree in house swapping from École Chalet in Basel, Switzerland. At the present time Ms. Rose is a freelance professional mourner who gets paid to attend the funerals of celebrities who have alienated all members of their family and any friends they'd once had.

Ms. Rose is the daughter of Charlene Rose of Andover, Massachusetts and Dr. Moises Rose of Novi Sad, Serbia. Her mother is a cymbal playing Scientologist who is the head coach of the Boston Pelicans, a woman's professional paintball team. Her father is the Josef Stalin Professor of Carnage and Despotism in the School of International Studies at Genocide University in Belgrade, Serbia. Ms. Rose is the stepdaughter of Irina Kvocich of Belgrade who breeds praying mantises and dodos.

Ms. Peppercorn, 42, who hires herself out as a personal chef and occasional dominatrix, has a degree in flapjack flipping and pancake mix whisking from the Institute of Culinary Arts in the former Yugoslavia, and a degree in mock turtle soups and salads from the Cultural Cooking Cooperative in Coeur d'Alene Idaho. She is the two time national wheelbarrow racing champion of Canada, and has published two award winning poetry collections, "Spirochetes in the Springtime" (Smooth Torso Press, 2008) and "Confessions of a Discolored Garden Gnome" (Confused Elf Books, 2010). Ms. Peppercorn had two previous marriages to men, both of which ended, one in divorce and the other as a result of suicide.

Ms. Peppercorn is the daughter of the late Myra Coons Peppercorn and Jeremiah Peppercorn. Her mother was a pioneer in the fields of anal bleaching and Brazilian waxing, and is thought to be one of the first estheticians to employ the French waxing style referred to as the "landing strip" in the United States. She was the vocal leader of a grassroots movement that recommended waxing as mechanism for eliminating pubic lice. Ms. Peppercorn's father is an inventor who has more than 20 patents registered in the United States Patent and Trademark Office. His best known invention is a pill that will render a person invisible for a period of 6 to 12 hours.

Ms. Peppercorn's great grandfather, Evert Peppercorn was a prominent barrister in London, England and a member of the House of Commons. According to "The Encyclopedia of Anomalous Events," her grandfather's death was the first recorded instance of a person dying as a result of spontaneous human combustion.

After a honeymoon in Brunei, where Ms. Peppercorn will compete in the International Wheelbarrow Racing Championships, the couple plan to live half the year in the Arctic Circle and the other half in Antarctica.

# Jose Jett and Melvin Morneau

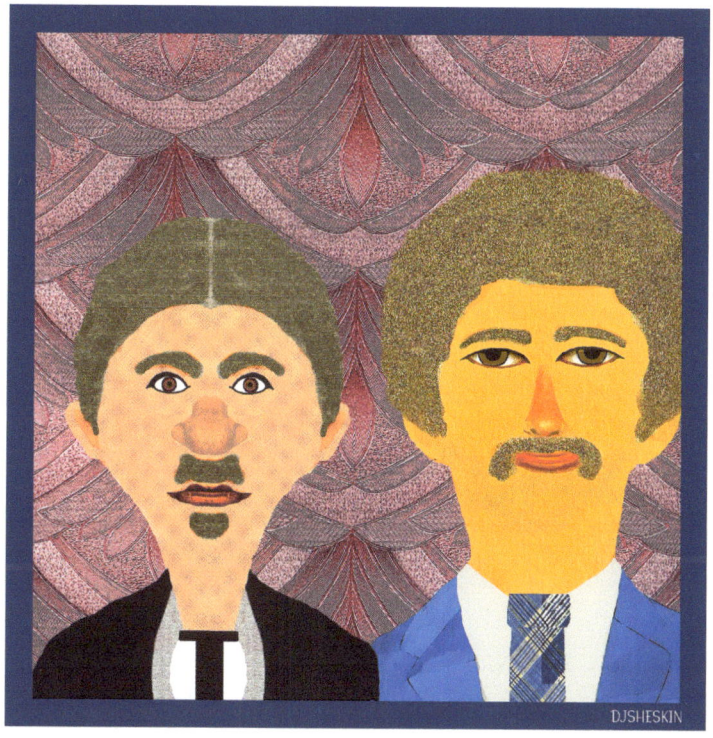

Jose Jett and Melvin Morneau were joined in holy matrimony August 11 in the Hall of Moans and Screams of the Museum of Unnatural History in Debased Gardens, Alabama. Afflicted with an acute episode of vertigo, as well as being mildly inebriated, The Right Revered Reid Rhoden, a former Facebook friend of Mr. Morneau, conducted the ceremony, aided by two strong lads who held on to each of his arms to prevent him from falling flat on his face.

Mr. Jett, 57, has a bachelor's degree in arcs and chords from The Institute of Tangents and Secants in Rectangle Falls, Oregon, a master's degree in parabolas and parallelograms from Rhombus University in Trapezoid, Delaware and a doctoral degree in cones and cylinders from The Octagon School of Acute Angles, in Obtuse, Ohio. In 2013 Mr. Jett retired from a fabulously successful 25 year career as a thumbtack and pushpin designer to fulfill a lifelong dream to become a grief counselor for people whose ant farms had been vandalized or destroyed by natural disasters. He is the author of two self-help books, "Triangular Breathing for Treating Convex Mood Swings" (Euclidian Geometrics Press, 2014) and "Equilateral Eye Movement Therapy for Concave Anger" (Cosine and Sons, 2016).

Mr. Jett is the son of the late Hazel and Maurice Jett. Mr. Jett's mother was a naturopathic healer who pioneered the use of octopus ink in the treatment of goose pimples and alerted the world to the value of squid ink in both stimulating and enhancing erotic daydreaming. His father was an accomplished grave robber who learned the trade in Italy when he was employed by the Italian army after the First World War to teach shell shocked soldiers how to play bocce ball.

Mr. Morneau, 43, who gravitated to the study of the unusual because of his mother's anatomical peculiarities, has a doctoral degree in Paleozoic perversions from Volcanic Ash University in Cretaceous, Colorado. At the present time he is the curator of mutations and sexual aberrations at the Museum of Unnatural History where he is the lead researcher in two seminal studies investigating the relationship between cannibalism and Vitamin K deficiency and the use of fish oil in treating necrophilia.

Mr. Morneau is the son of the late Catherine and Phillipe Morneau. His mother, who had four nipples and only one eye in the center of her head, was a unicycle rider with Cirque du Soleil for 14 years. She died in 1998 during a performance as a result of an allergic reaction to a lubricant that had been applied to the chain of her bike. Mr. Morneau's father, who was an appraiser of precious stones, gallstones and kidney stones, was a nitrous oxide enthusiast who died from uncontrollable laughing while he was under sedation during a routine root canal.

Mr. Jett and Mr. Morneau met in 2014 through the dating app Geometry Meets Paleontology.

# Nancy Mandella and Carl Schwarz

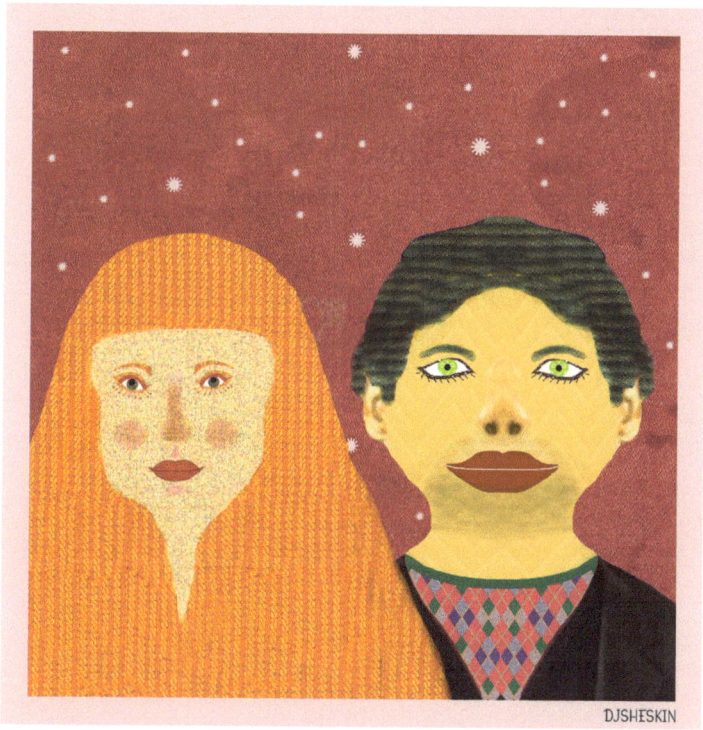

DJSHESKIN

Nancy Mandella and Carl Schwarz were married August 22 in a hot air balloon positioned directly above the Old Faithful geyser in Yellowstone National Park, Wyoming. The ceremony was jointly officiated by Willem Pennsaugen, a biracial, involuntarily celibate Quaker pastor who was a former prom date of Ms. Mandella, and Dr. Meredith Chu, a sex therapist and former surrogate sex partner of Mr. Schwarz, who was ordained as a connubial officiant for the event by the National Park Service. To add to the excitement of the day, in the middle of the ceremony Old Faithful unexpectedly erupted sending a mist of steaming water up into the air. Fifteen minutes later a drenched but elated bride and groom landed safely in a clearing to be greeted by 150 well-wishers and Smokey the Bear.

The bride, 20, who describes herself as a fiery, fair-skinned, freckled red head, is currently in her senior year at the Tattletale Institute of Gossip and Chitchat in Grapevine, Georgia where she is majoring in dirty laundry and hearsay. She is due to graduate at the end of the fall semester when she completes her senior thesis entitled "Sometimes a Rumor Can Be Worse than a Tumor." During the past three summers she has been an intern and undercover snoop for the tabloid publication the National Enquirer. Ms. Mandella also plays the harp in the popular all girl heavy metal band "Bitches that Snitch."

Ms. Mandella is the daughter of Arlene and Delsin Mandella of Savanah, Georgia. The bride's mother designs bikinis for chimpanzees that participate in aquatic themed movies and online videos. Her father is a money launderer for South American drug cartels and a spokesman for corrupt European politicians.

The groom, 28, is an honors graduate of the University of Enumeration in Tartu, Estonia. He is currently on assignment as a consultant from the United States Department of Interior to the European Union, where his major responsibilities are counting and cataloging the number of feet on Eastern European centipedes and millipedes, and determining the feasibility of designing ergonomic footwear for the latter multi legged species. Mr. Schwarz, who freely admits to having a fierce freckle fetish, is also a freckle scientist who is available for hire to count the number of freckles on a person's face. He is also regularly employed as a judge in freckle frequency competitions.

Mr. Schwarz is the son of Sadie and Samson Schwarz of Coos Bay, Oregon. The groom's mother is a volunteer pet sitter in the Pacific Northwest for individuals who are serving prison sentences of six months or less. The groom's father, who is retired, was formerly employed by the United States Coast Guard as a foghorn tuner. At the present time he is employed by the United States Postal Service to deliver chain letters and defused letter bombs.

The couple met when a friend of the bride emailed her that someone by the name of Carl Schwarz posted online that he was involved in a sexual relationship with a psycho nymphomaniac named Nancy Mandella. When Ms. Mandella confronted the groom on Facebook she discovered that it was a case of mistaken identity, and in fact the person making false claims about her was a reclusive cactus farmer from Roswell, New Mexico by the name of Carl Schwartz who, to the best of her recollection, she had refused to kiss during a game of Spin the Bottle when she was in the ninth grade. After their initial contact Ms. Mandella and the groom quickly became Facebook friends, and four months later officially announced that they had become a couple.

# Marissa Bosanova and Lebron Paz Cortes

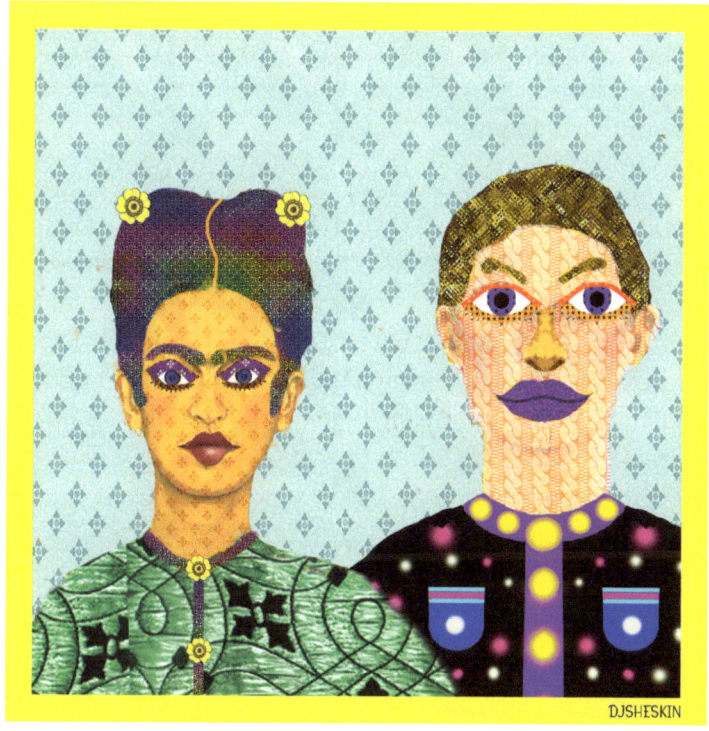

**D**uring an Ayahuasca retreat attended by 52 pilgrims who had accompanied them on a journey below the Equator in search of wisdom and healing, Marissa Bosanova and Lebron Paz Cortes were married on September 5 in an Amazon rainforest in Eastern Peru. As they and their fellow pilgrims drank from a brew made out of ayahuasca vine and the leaves of the chacruna plant, the couple was guided through their vows by the Shipibo cultural shaman Xiripstwo. The four hour ceremony, punctuated with episodic chanting, howling, vomiting and dancing, culminated at sundown with all parties collapsing to the ground in a state of ecstasy and total exhaustion.

The bride, 29, who is thought to be the biological daughter of indigenous Amazon Indians, was born and abandoned in a rainforest in Southwest Brazil. She was discovered in infancy by an itinerant priest who entrusted her to a honeymooning couple who had journeyed to the Amazon basin to swim with piranhas and commune with the forest people. Although she lived in the Midwestern United States for many years, after her parents divorced Ms. Bosanova moved to Mexico where she attended the University of Biological Sciences in Acapulco from which she received a bachelor's degree in visionary psychedelics. She subsequently obtained a doctoral degree in shamanic medicine from Curare University in São Luis, Brazil, where she is presently employed as an Assistant Professor in the department of voodoo studies and head shrinking.

Ms. Bosanova is the daughter of Astrid Bosanova of Des Moines, Iowa and Carlos Bosanova of Vera Cruz, Mexico. Ms. Bosanova's mother, who is a part-time cook in Des Moines for Meals on Wheels, is the only independent party whose cooking has been awarded a Michelin star rating. She is also an accomplished long distance swimmer and recreational deep sea diver who announced last year that during a marathon swim in the Pacific Ocean she had discovered a new continent submerged at the bottom of a massive underwater canyon 950 miles off the coast of Southern Chile. The bride's father is a professional actor who for 35 years has played the role of the snake in the award winning Mexican soap opera "Adam and Eve," and has recently been cast in the role of Satan in the forthcoming television drama "The Devil Has Diarrhea."

The groom, 32, has an associate's degree in hypoallergenic baking from The Institute of Éclairs and Macarons, in Lyons, France. He is CEO of Savory Tarts and Poison Darts, a company that prepares pastries for celebratory events and sells strychnine and curare tipped darts to professional assassins and headhunters.

The groom is the son of Mira Paz and Antonio Cortes of Lima, Peru. The groom's mother is a breeder of Bombay cats, a shorthair breed of domestic black cat. She also has a part-time practice as a mental health counselor which she devotes exclusively to the treatment of people who have a fear of black cats. The groom's father is a passion fruit farmer who has a side business repairing damaged Ouija boards.

The couple met in 2013 when they were almost 5000 miles apart (she in Brazil, he in France) experimenting with the synthetic hallucinatory drug PCP (phencyclidine). As Ms. Bosanova and Mr. Paz Cortes recollect, they simultaneously experienced hallucinations in which the other person's face along with contact information materialized followed by an incisive directive from a higher power to search one another out. Which, happily, they did.

# Hazel Braun and Fred Hotz

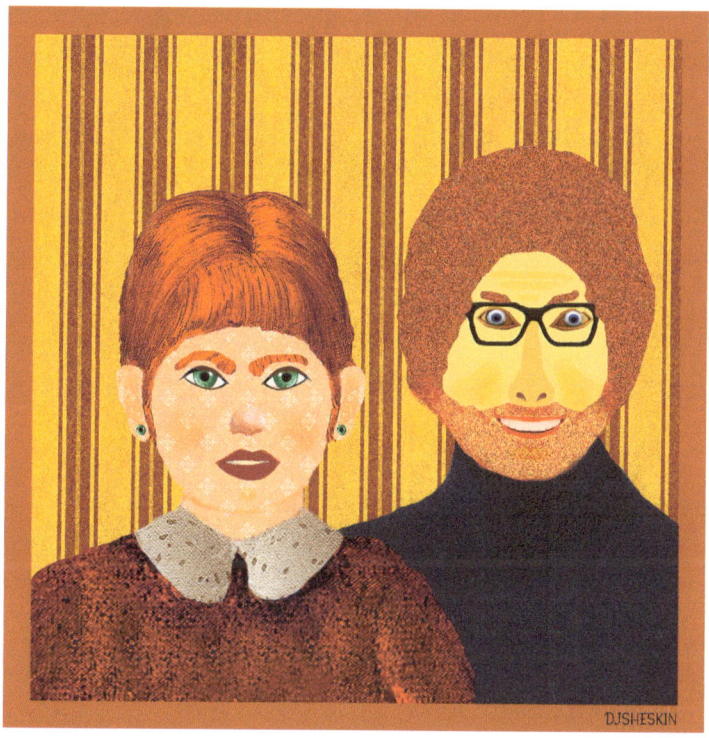

**H**azel Zadie Braun and Fred Hotz were married September 22 in an impromptu ceremony at an undisclosed location in Djibouti, Africa. The event was officiated by His Majesty Barnabas IV, the deposed dictator of Djibouti, who was a close friend of the groom's father. Immediately after the ceremony the couple, accompanied by the King, who had been granted asylum by the Republic of Venezuela, flew to Caracas in His Majesty's private plane.

The bride, 26, is a former debutante who came out at the age of 18 at the 58th Annual International Debutante's Ball in New York. She is the owner of Perfumed Donkey, an appointment only boutique in Caracas that sells aromatic scents and aphrodisiacs for barnyard animals that are being groomed for mating. Ms. Braun is an honors graduate of The Libido Institute in Vulvavolcano, Venezuela with a degree in pheromone science.

The bride is the daughter of Millicent Rockefeller Braun of Mount

Vernon, New York and Marcel Braun, who is currently residing in Leavenworth Kansas. Ms. Braun's mother, who claims to be the great-great granddaughter of John D. Rockefeller, is a philanthropist who is listed in New York Magazine as one of the top 50 socialites in the world. She is the author of the best-selling memoir "I Hate My Nose, I Hate My Daughter, I Hate My Orthodontist! " (Animosity Press, 2012). The bride's father is serving a 25 year prison sentence at the United States Penitentiary in Leavenworth Kansas for loan sharking and kidnapping. During his time in prison, where he works in the automotive shop, he has become something of a celebrity artist for creating unusual three dimensional works of art in his spare time out of automobile timing belts, fan belts and garter belts (that are sent to him by a former mistress) that his daughter sells on eBay.

The groom, 30, who has a bachelor's degree in finance from the Wharton School of Business, is a money launderer for the continents of South America and Africa. He is a former All-American soccer player who played professionally for two years in Europe before he was forced to retire as a result of sustaining a life threatening injury to his ego when he became incontinent as he executed a sudden death penalty shootout kick during a World Cup semifinal match.

The groom is the son of Marsha Hotz of Hackensack, New Jersey and the late Samuel "Smiley" Hotz. The groom's mother describe herself as the world's only "graphic philosopher" — specifically, for a modest fee, using her pinkie finger she engraves an aphorism or witticism in a slab of pastel tinted wet cement that once hardened she custom frames to be hung inside a client's house. The groom's late father was a professional criminal who was convicted in 2007 by the United States Federal Government of money laundering. He was serving a 15 year sentence at the United States Penitentiary in Otisville, New York when he was stabbed to death with a chicken bone by a fellow inmate during an argument in the prison cafeteria over the size of a serving of fish sticks.

The couple first met in 2004 during a volleyball game at a picnic sponsored by the heads of organized crime families in the Eastern United States.

# Elspeth Woo and Christian Pretty

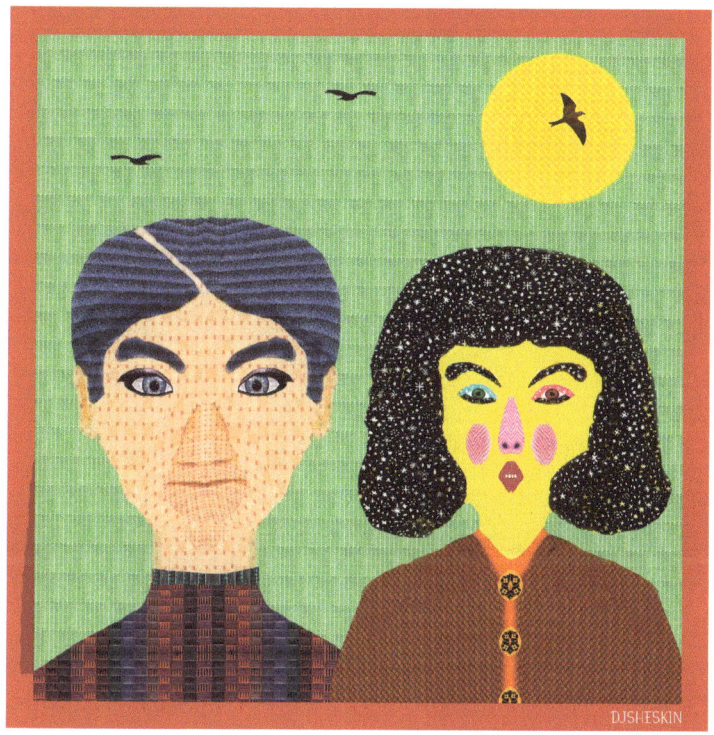

Elspeth Nicolette Woo and Christian Pretty were married October 1 at Our Lady of the Cross Catholic Church in Locust Valley, Missouri. Father Malachi McCordless, a Roman Catholic priest, officiated. One month prior to the ceremony in a rented house outside of St. Louis, Father McCordless performed a three day exorcism on the groom during which a malevolent demon that had been haunting Mr. Pretty for 13 and one half years was expelled and banished for eternity to a sealed culvert along the banks of the Mississippi River.

The bride, 39, has been employed since 2007 by the Papal Basilica of St. Peter in the Vatican where she supervises nuns and priests who have been assigned to shred confidential documents the Catholic Church does not want made public. She is an honors graduate of the Institute of Pontifical Secrets in Venice, Italy from which she has a Doctor of Spiritual Science degree in skullduggery and the science of expurgation and extermination.

Ms. Woo, who for as long as she can remember has always been a fan of rare and undercooked beef, is a two-time mad cow disease survivor.

The bride is the daughter of Portia Woo of Cairo, Egypt and the late Hiram Woo. The bride's mother is a toll collector at the Suez Canal. Her late father was a university trained professional agitator and skilled projectile thrower who sold his services as an aggressor in Third World riots. He was fatally wounded in 2006 while throwing rocks at Israeli soldiers during a Palestinian uprising at the Gaza Strip.

The groom, 35, who is the only one-legged bounty hunter in the state of Missouri, is a magna cum laude graduate of Carbine University in Ballistic Bay, Wyoming where he earned a bachelor of arts degree in muzzle velocity. Mr. Pretty is a regular contributor to *American Rifleman*, the official journal of the National Rifle Association. He is the author of "Bumper Stocks or Argyle Socks" (Black Powder Press, 2014), a lavishly illustrated coffee table book that debates the pros and cons of collecting firearms versus footwear.

The groom is the son of Alicia and Fenwick Pretty of Hamburg, Germany. The groom's mother is an avant-garde artist who creates costume jewelry and infant mobiles by using mutilated scarecrows, discarded toe nail clippings and remnant adult diapers. The groom's father is the owner of a construction company that builds moats around the castles of the aristocracy which he stocks with alligators and other man eating species.

The couple met in 2016 in Madagascar when the groom was run over by a full terrain vehicle while he was canoodling on a beach with woman he had just met, and Ms. Woo, who happened to be sunbathing a few yards from the amorous couple, saved Mr. Pretty's life by applying dressings to his groin and a tourniquet to his bleeding left leg which subsequently had to be amputated.

# Cristina Paloma Oostermann and Ira Rollert

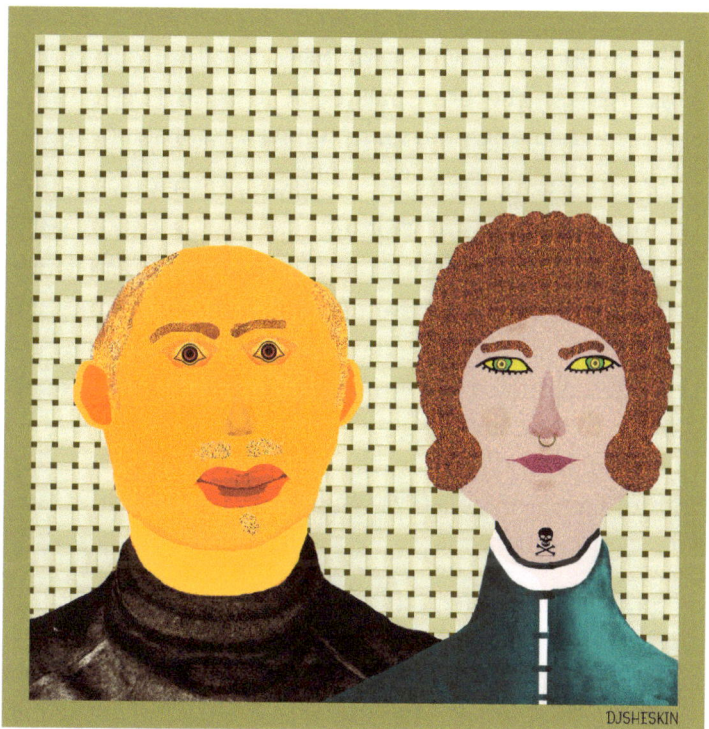

Cristina Paloma Oostermann and Ira Rollert were married October 17 on the lawn of Miss Pearl's Bed and Breakfast in Sagebrush, Texas. The ceremony was performed by Hermes Candland, the godfather of the bride who is a Unitarian minister who for the past eight years has been in the United States Federal Witness Protection Program as a result of him testifying in a murder-for-hire case orchestrated by a Mexican drug cartel.

The couple met 18 months ago when the groom was designated as the bride's probation officer following her release from the Texas State Penitentiary at Huntsville where she was incarcerated five years for assault with a deadly weapon. Under the terms of her probation she will have to wear an ankle bracelet 24 hours a day and, for better or for worse, report to her probation officer-husband once a week.

For the past year the bride, 33, has been a professional roller derby player for the Tijuana Mexico Assassins competing under the name of Pain Eyre.

Ms. Oostermann, who admits to being both a kleptomaniac and borderline nymphomaniac, has been arrested on multiple occasions since the year 2000 for a broad variety of criminal offenses that include assault with a deadly weapon, manslaughter burglary, domestic violence, stalking and vandalism. She has only been convicted of assault with a deadly weapon and domestic violence, for which she has served time in both state and federal penitentiaries. The bride has been married previously, with her two former husbands dying under suspicious circumstances.

The bride is the daughter of Danni Oostermann of Stockholm, Sweden and the late Nils Oostermann. The bride's mother retired in 2010 as a professional boxer with a record of 56 wins, 4 losses and 1 draw. From 1991 to 1997 she was the middleweight champion of Europe, and in 1998 won the world middleweight championship which she held until 2002. Since 2003 she has modeled lingerie for full figured women and sold taser guns and hormone free chewing gum online. The bride's father is a former professional wrestler who went by the ring name Bludyard Crippling. He died of a brain aneurysm in 2009 while participating in a Japanese tea ceremony in Kyoto, Japan.

The groom, 54, is a probation officer for the state of Texas. He is a graduate of the Institute of Crime and Punishment in Raskolnikov, Indiana where he was awarded a bachelor's degree in Russian literature and a master's degree in first degree murder. The title of his senior thesis, which won an award as the best forensic paper in Eastern Europe, was "Shoplifting as a Gateway Crime to High Treason."

The groom is the son of Bertha Rollert and General Samson Rollert of Fayetteville, Arkansas. The groom's mother is a televangelist who goes by the name Joan of Arkansas and is the owner of the cable television network KJAK. The groom's father, now retired, was a brigadier general in the United States Armed Forces serving in the Judge Advocate General's Corps where his major responsibility was overseeing the prosecution of cases involving the theft of protein products and buttermilk from military kitchens.

# Kezia Alagash and Pietro Sgru

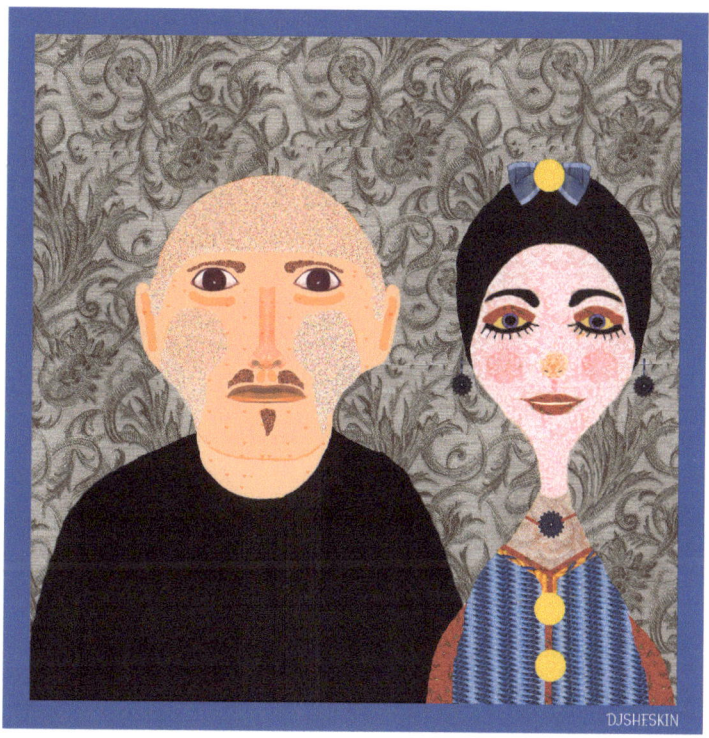

DJSHESKIN

**K**ezia Alagash and Dr. Pietro Sgru were married October 24 on Pier 84 overlooking the Hudson River in lower Manhattan. The Gypsy elder Vlax Ziko presided over a Romani ceremony in which Doctors Ian and Regina Bobbit, board certified oral and maxillofacial surgeons granted one-day solemnization certificates by the State of New York, introduced Catholic axioms and Jewish postulates into the couple's vows.

The bride, 19, is a Roma gypsy, who is the youngest of eight children of a nomadic Romani couple that emigrated to the United States from Croatia in 1994. In September Ms. Alagash will begin studying for an online nomadic degree in green tea leaf reading and crystal ball juggling at the Roma Institute of Occult Studies in Necromancy, Nebraska.

The bride is the daughter of Mala and Samiel Alagash who are senior members of a Gypsy caravan that travels throughout the Eastern United States. The bride's mother is an accomplished fortune teller and palm reader who has advised two Vice Presidents, 126 Senators, three Super Bowl winning quarterbacks and 11 Academy Award winning actors or actresses. The bride's father is a former hedge fund manager for Goldman Sachs who was indicted in 2016 by the Securities and Exchange Commission for making an illegal right turn at a red light on the corner of 49th Street and 5th Avenue.

The groom, 45, is a former board certified oral and maxillofacial surgeon who abandoned dental medicine in 2016 to enroll in a master's degree program at the Grift Institute in Seascam, South Carolina from which he will graduate in June with a degree in fraud and deceit. Upon graduation Dr. Sgru plans to become a professional pickpocket on the corner of 5th Avenue and 49th Street.

The groom is the son of Vanessa and Stanley Sgru of Denton, Texas. The groom's mother is a naturopathic physician who is a vocal advocate of utilizing parasitic worms in the treatment of obesity. She is currently leading a campaign to designate August 14 as Tapeworm Appreciation Day. The groom's father is a nationally certified urine testing monitor employed by four professional sports leagues. During the past decade he has observed over 10,000 professional athletes pee into a cup.

The couple met in 2015 when the groom came to consult the bride's mother for a palm reading and was advised to abandon dental medicine and, instead, utilize his nimble fingers and exceptional fine hand coordination to pick people's pockets.

# Holly Micheletti and Wendell Smite

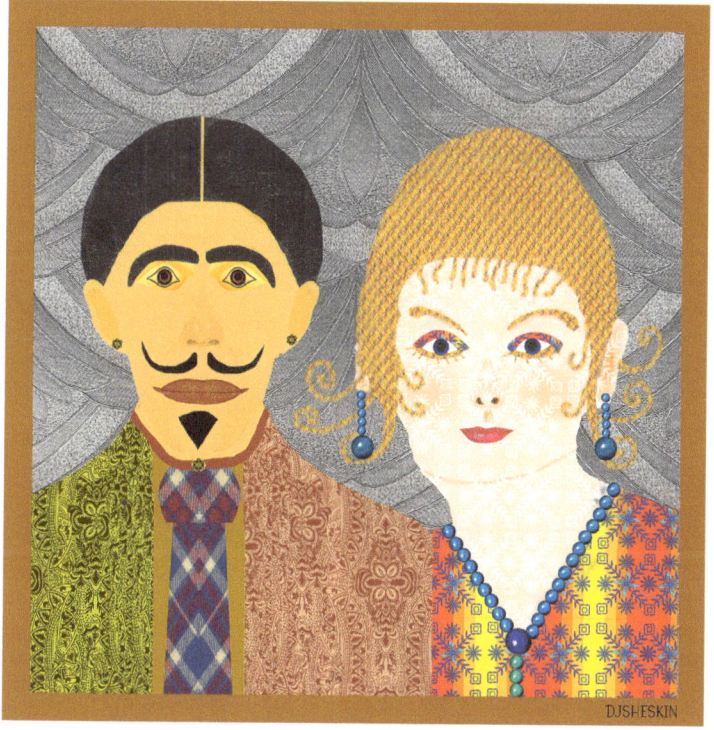

**H**olly Marissa Micheletti and Wendell Cohoes Smite were married November 7 along the banks of Middle Elk Creek in Buchanan County, Virginia. The ceremony was supervised by the harlequin romance writer and drag queen Ivory Snow, who had declared herself to be Queen for a Day. Heather Pollock Polk, Ms. Micheletti's identical twin sister who was separated at birth from the bride but reunited last year, augmented the occasion by periodically inserting quotes from the abdication speech of King Edward VIII into the couple's vows.

The bride, 36, has a bachelor's degree in reticence and a master's degree in quiescence from Echoless University in Hush-Hush, Minnesota where she is an adjunct professor in the department of silence. She is a fierce advocate of "covert inaudible communication," which teaches both children and adults how to eye blink in Morse code in lieu of everyday conversation, as well as the use of eye-blink Morse code as a subtle but effective way of alerting members of the general public to imminent danger.

The bride is the daughter of Marison Micheletti of Silver Springs, West Virginia and the late Harrison Micheletti. The bride's mother is the owner of Dirty Fingers, a company that specializes in manufacturing soap for washing the hands of mute children who are caught cursing using sign language. The bride's late father was the founder and director of a sanctuary for endangered animal species that were caught eating endangered plant species. He died in 2010 from an aggressive case of poison oak he contracted when he was foraging for discarded crack vials in a neglected meadow adjacent to his sanctuary.

The groom, 45, is an award winning playwright who was the recipient of a MacArthur Genius Award in 2002. In 2006 he won the Pulitzer Prize for Drama for his play "The Uncircumcised Bail Bondsman" Mr. Smite is also a professional drag queen who began crossdressing at the age of 12. He is a graduate of Audacious University in Cheeky, Delaware where he received degrees in brazen behavior and unrestrained histrionics.

The groom is the son of Audrey and Austin Smite of Orem, Utah. His mother has a doctoral degree in osculation from the Institute of Caressing and Embracing in Smooch, Tennessee where she is an adjunct professor in the department of kissing and cuddling. She is also a nationally syndicated advice columnist who is a vocal advocate of employing glucosamine and chondroitin to prevent the accumulation of belly button lint. Mr. Smite's father, who has 24 body piercings and is double jointed, is a bookmaker who only takes bets on ostrich racing and the date of celebrity deaths.

The couple met in 2013 at a silence and body rebalancing retreat for drag queens in which the bride had been invited to blink advice to those in search of peace and tranquility.

# Purity Basquiat and Mario Infurious

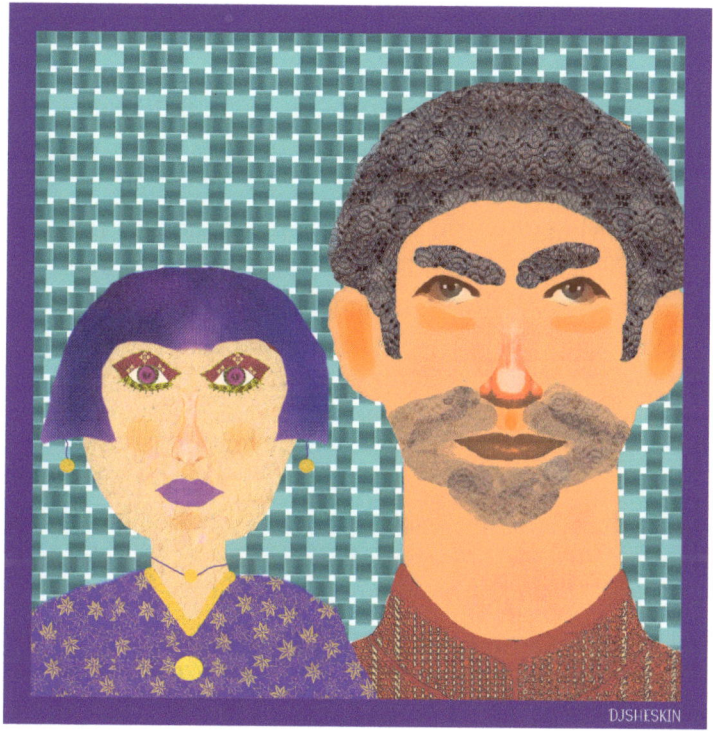

Purity Basquiat and Mario Carlos Infurious were married November 16 in the garden of the Marshall Tito Psychoanalytic Institute in Podgorica, Montenegro. Although a Catholic priest was present to satisfy statutory and ecclesiastical requirements, the ceremony was conducted autonomously with the couple reciting their vows to one another — albeit, the groom's vows were punctuated with embarrassing and occasionally offensive Freudian slips.

The bride, 23, was born and raised in Madrid, Spain. Upon reaching the age of 17 she emancipated herself from her parents and moved to New York City to become a sport groupie and pursue her dream of becoming a graffiti artist. In 2014 she legally changed her last name to that of her idol Jean-Michel Basquiat, and enrolled in the Art Students League of New York where for two years she studied doodling and urban defacement. Between 2015 and 2017 her chalk art could be regularly found on the sidewalks of

Manhattan below 14<sup>th</sup> Street. In 2017 Ms. Basquiat moved to Montenegro, where she occasionally paints graffiti on the walls of public buildings, to live with Mr. Infurious.

The bride is the daughter of Miranda Palmeri-Astacio and her wife Evanescent Palmeri-Astacio, both residents of Madrid, Spain. Miranda Palmeri-Astacio, who was impregnated by an anonymous male sperm donor, is the bride's biological mother with her wife Evanescent Palmeri-Astacio listed as a second mother on Ms. Basquiat's birth certificate. The Palmeri-Astacio's are the owners of Time is Precious, a timekeeping company, where Miranda, who is a glassblower, creates hourglasses that Evanescent fills with sand. The two women also build and calibrate sundials. Evanescent Palmeri-Astacio has an independent practice as a needle-in-a haystack-finder, and is one of only ten people in all of Europe who are certified as grandmasters in the latter profession.

The groom 33, who is seven feet four inches tall, is a professional basketball player in Europe where he is currently under contract with the Montenegro Motherfxckers. Mr. Infurious played one year of college basketball at the University of Kentucky where he was the first round draft choice of the New York Knickerbockers in the annual draft of the National Basketball Association. After playing five years for the Knickerbockers, because of accusations of sexual assault against him, Mr. Infurious elected to move to Montenegro (which does not have an extradition treaty to the United States) to continue his professional basketball career.

The groom is the son of Salma and Humberto Infurious who currently reside in New York City. The groom's mother is a crisis and hostage negotiator for the New York City Police Department. Her specialty is defusing situations that have a potential for domestic or workplace violence by using pastries, candy, and eggnog as incentives to dissuade potential perpetrators from engaging in destructive behavior. The groom's father is employed by the United States Securities and Exchange Commission where he uses aromatherapy, soothing music and sugar free confections to reduce the level of hostility in hostile takeovers.

The couple met during the 2016 Summer Olympics in Rio de Janeiro, Brazil when the groom became smitten with the bride at an invitation only orgy for jumbo sized athletes and professional groupies.

# Erin Hyacinth Finch and
# Errol Chartres Flynn

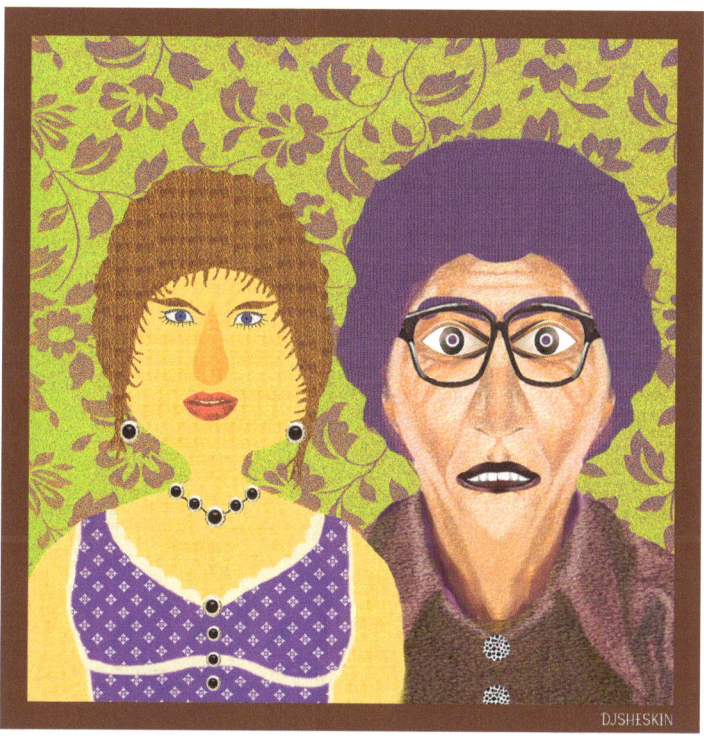

Erin Hyacinth Finch and Errol Chartres Flynn were married December 24 in Newport, Rhode Island on the back lawn of the Finch Mansion that borders the Cliff Walk and overlooks the Atlantic Ocean. Reverend Aubrey Arnold III, a spiritualist and born again agnostic, officiated the event. A number of people present at the ceremony stated that as Ms. Finch was reciting her vows her deceased maternal great grandfather Olen Fallon Worthington materialized alongside her and dabbed the tears of joy that flowed from the bride's eyes with a diaphanous silk handkerchief.

The bride, 47, is a luxury sex toy designer for women who sells gold and platinum plated dildos, vibrators and Ben Wa balls to an elite clientele. Ms. Finch is a graduate of Finch College in Manhattan where she majored in cotillion studies and nuclear physics. Prior to designing sex toys she worked surreptitiously for the United States Atomic Energy Commission where she was responsible for purchasing uranium and plutonium on the black market to stockpile for potential use in nuclear weapons. The bride had three previous marriages, the last two of which ended in divorce. Her first husband died as a result of radiation poisoning.

The bride is the daughter of Selma and Caleb Finch of Newport. The bride's mother is prominent socialite and well-known animal advocate who achieved notoriety in 2001 when she roller skated across the United States dressed as an opossum to protest animal cruelty. Ms. Finch's father is a retired used car salesman whose was fined $10,000 in 1995 by the state of Rhode Island and forced to retire for rolling back the mileage on automobile odometers. Since his retirement he has been engaged in building the world's tallest ladder out of recycled rubbish on the back lawn of the Finch family mansion that to date extends 6,500 feet into the sky.

The groom 52, is a celebrity plumber who over the past three decades has unclogged and repaired the toilets of the rich and famous. For 24 years he has been the star of the Emmy award winning syndicated television show "These Pipes Are Not for Smoking." In 2006 Mr. Flynn was selected as Time Magazine's Man of the Year. The groom is a widower, who in accordance with his deceased wife's wishes froze her brain cryogenically for possible revival in the future.

The groom is the son of Carolyn Flynn of Boston and the late Marshal Flynn. The groom's mother is a legendary former dumpster diver who over a 25 year period retrieved what is estimated to be over forty million dollars' worth of salvageable waste from commercial, residential and industrial construction containers. Since her retirement in 2015 she has been an inner city volunteer who has mentored over 250 derelicts and slackers, teaching them how by using common sense and stealth one can both survive and thrive in urban America. The groom's late father, who at one point weighed over 600 pounds, was a sumo wrestler in Japan for over two decades. Upon returning to the United States he became a successful competitive eater who choked to death in 2006 during a competition while he was attempting to break the world record for the number of lemon meringue pies a person could eat in an hour.

The couple met through the dating app Rauch Meets Wrench.

# Mercy Meyers and Orin Oliphant

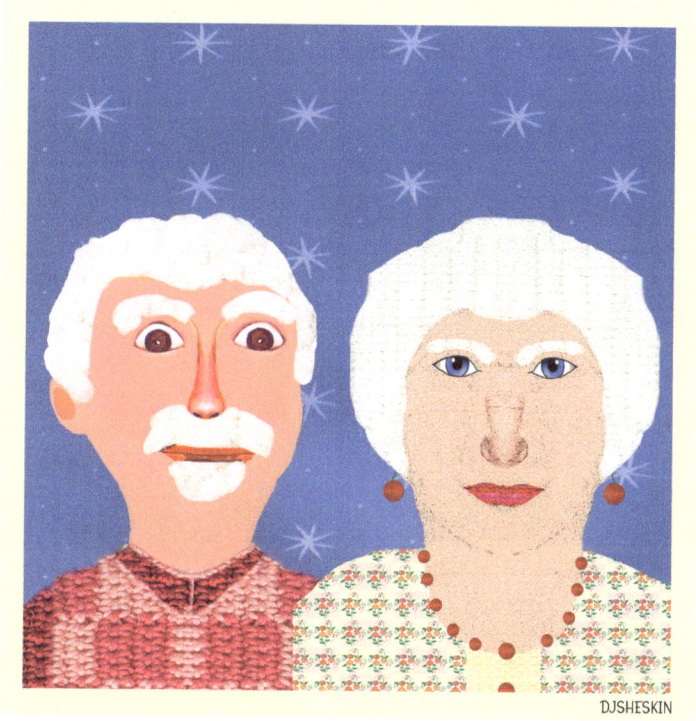

DJSHESKIN

Mercy Magellan Meyers and Orin Oliphant were married December 31 in an ultraorthodox Jewish ceremony March 23 in front of the Western Wailing Wall in the Old City of Jerusalem, Israel. The groom's younger brother Myron Oliphant, 92, officiated, having become a Rabbi for the Day thorough the auspices of the Torah Society of Eurasia. The bride was supported during the ceremony by her kosher Vietnamese miniature pot-bellied pig, Matzo Ball, who she held onto throughout the ceremony with a short leash to prevent him from attacking the groom, with whom in the past he had issues relating to jealousy and Mr. Oliphant's addiction to pork rinds.

The bride, 98, who converted to Judaism at the age of 82, is a former ballerina, musician and opera singer who performed throughout Europe and the United States during a career that spanned 43 years. In the summer of 1940, on sabbatical from studying ballet at the Julliard School of Dance in New York City, while hitchhiking across the United States Ms. Meyers met and married her first husband, the famous Irish Traveler Gypsy folk hero, Luther Boorag. During her time with Mr. Boorag the couple provided entertainment at Gypsy weddings and bar mitzvahs with Ms. Meyers serenading Mr. Boorag on the fiddle while he wrestled a grizzly bear. After Mr. Boorag sustained fatal injuries at a bar mitzvah in Wheeling, West Virginia, Ms. Meyers returned to Julliard where she completed her formal education. She subsequently had three other marriages, all of which ended in divorce, albeit they did result in five children — two sons and three daughters, all of whom perished in tsunamis or volcanic eruptions. Among the venues the bride either danced or sang at during her illustrious career are the Vienna State Opera, the Bolshoi Theater, the Royal Opera of Versailles and the Metropolitan Opera House in New York.

The bride is the daughter of the late Doris and Hyman Myers. The bride's mother was a seamstress who purchased and resized for resale bridal gowns from brides who had been jilted at the altar. Her father was a professional gambler and pizza deliveryman, who during the Second World War was part of the flight crew that dropped an atomic bomb on Nagasaki on April 9, 1945,

The bride's maternal grandfather, Freddy "Speedy" Flegg, worked as a Pony Express rider and stagecoach driver for Leavenworth and Pike's Peak Express Company. Her paternal grandfather, Evander Meyers, was hung by the neck until he was dead in Denton, Texas in 1869 for cattle rustling. Both of Ms. Meyers grandmothers worked as saloon dancers and part-time prostitutes, one in Abilene, Texas and the other in Cheyenne, Wyoming.

The groom, 101, who converted to Judaism at the age of 99, has a doctoral degree in psychology from Harvard University. He was an acclaimed scholar for many years (working at such prestigious universities as Stanford, Yale, Princeton and Columbia) until he was expelled from academia for plagiarizing large sections of his influential and highly praised book "Fidgeting, Whistling and Flirting in Precocious Infants" (Crybaby Books, 1954). He reinvented himself in 1960 by obtaining a position as a rest room attendant at the Plaza Hotel in New York City during which time he made a good living from the generous tips he received from the hotel's exclusive clientele, and also became privy to high society gossip and scandal which resulted in him writing the best-selling book "Toilet Tabloid" (Overflow Press, 1979). The groom had two previous marriages, both of which ended when his wives were murdered, one time by terrorists the other by one of Mr. Oliphant's mistresses.

The groom is the son of the late Gertrude and Ezra Oliphant. The groom's mother was a fashion award winning buttonhole designer who was a life-long hypochondriac. The groom's father was a drinking companion and confidante of L. Ron Hubbard, the founder of Scientology. Although the groom's father had a successful career as quill and fur farmer, during which time he raised porcupines, chinchillas, caterpillars and hedgehogs, he is probably best remembered for being an advocate of late life circumcision as a mechanism for prolonging the sex drive of aging uncircumcised males.

The bride and groom first met at a wake in 1987. They subsequently ran into one another over a 30 year period at what they estimate to be over 100 funerals. Last year they decided it was cheaper to get married than to absorb the expense of separately attending any future funerals.

# See-!rainity Ice and Cuoco Empos

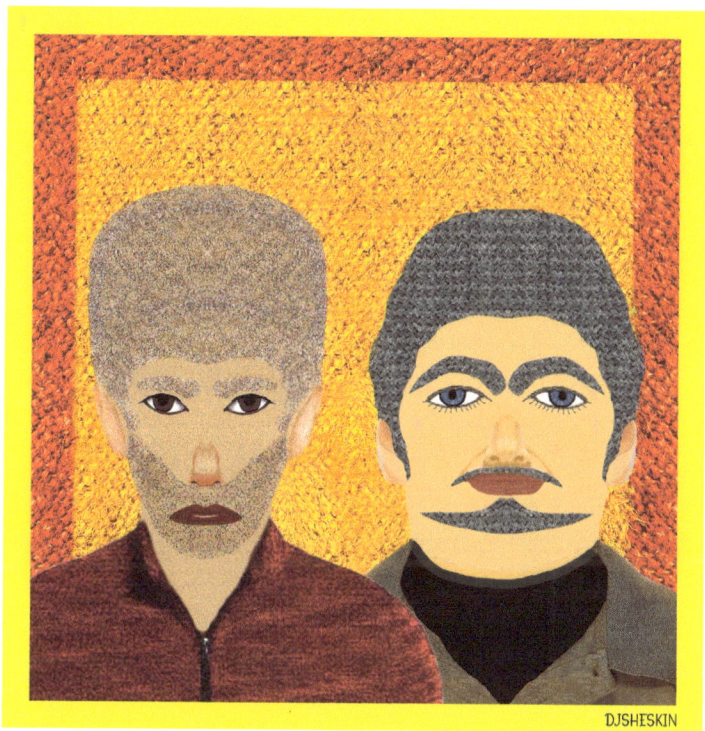

DJSHESKIN

At 11:59 PM on December 31, the suntanned heavily-muscled life coach Paulson Van Dever, who had been certified for the day by the Association of Nude Dudes as an au naturale priest, joined Professor See-!rainity Ice and Cuoco Empos in holy matrimony. Without anyone in attendance wearing a stitch of clothing, the couple exchanged vows and simultaneously committed to a lifestyle that accommodated both nudity and unrestrained personal expression. At the conclusion of the ceremony a bonfire was erected into which all parties present tossed the garments they had been forced to wear by a prim and uninformed society in order to transport themselves to what they considered to be a sacred and naked moment in their lives.

See-!rainity Ice, 44, is an award winning photographer who is renowned for his images of dust, fog, tailpipe exhaust, blood stains and human auras. He is a graduate of Aperture University in Shutter Speed, Montana with degrees in blurry imaging and bounce flashing. He is a professor and the chairman of the department of photographic imaging and human relations at Colorimeter College in Halftone, Maine where, among other things, he teaches courses in spirit photography, time lapse pornography and imaging human emotions. Professor Ice is the author of the exquisite coffee table book "The Dust Bunny: That Enigmatic Entanglement of Dead Skin, Spider Webs, Dust, Light Rubbish and Debris Held Together by Static Electricity" (Achoo Press, 1999) and the best-selling memoir "A Scandalous History of Overexposure: My Life Inside the Darkroom and Outside the Bedroom" (Red Eye Publications, 2015).

Mr. Ice is the son of Violet Ice of Kokomo, Indiana and the late Percy Ice. His mother, who since reaching the age of majority has believed that by staring at the sun one can learn to communicate with single-celled organisms, lost her sight in 2005 as a result of looking directly at the sun during a partial solar eclipse. Since losing her sight she has mastered braille in 14 different languages and is the director of a clinic that trains amoeba and anaerobic bacteria to play chess and do origami. Mr. Ice's father was a red carpet weaver who for more than 20 years wove the red carpets that celebrities walked on during special events. For most of his adult life, ostensibly to protect himself from germs, he wore a full face mask in public. However, after his death it was discovered that he had been hiding his identity because he was wanted by the authorities for starting over 100 fires over a thirty year period that had resulted in more than 100 million dollars' worth of property damage and the deaths of over 500 people.

Mr. Cuoco, 37, who has the word MOMMY tattooed on his penis, recruits people to sell their kidneys, liver and lungs for transplant into other human beings. Due to a rare genetic condition the aroma of Mr. Cuoco's bodily fluids have aphrodisiacal properties, and because of the latter he regularly sell his blood, tears and urine on the black market for use as moisturizer, perfume and sunscreen.

Mr. Cuoco is the son of the late Luciana and Mateo Cuoco. His mother was a professional juror who offered her services to people who did not want to serve on jury duty. She was fatally wounded at the conclusion of a trial in 2002 by an enraged defendant who had been convicted of stealing his neighbor's junk mail. Mr. Cuoco's father was a world renowned polymath who is believed to be the inspiration for the "most interesting man in the world" character depicted in Dos Equis beer commercials. Among other things, he was reputed to be regularly questioned by the police for the simple reason that they found him to be fascinating, and on more than one occasion he was invited to art museums such as the Metropolitan Museum of Art and the Louvre where he was asked to modify the paintings of old masters to be more to his liking. He died in 2013 when he shot himself in the head while he was playing a game of Russian roulette with a fully loaded gun.

Professor Ice and Mr. Cuoco met at a blood and dust seminar for nudists sponsored by the the American Red Cross and the International Association of Dust and Debris. Mr. Cuoco was lecturing on the subject of nonconsensual bloodletting and Mr. Ice was displaying images of bloodstains he had photographed that are now utilized within the field of clinical psychology as a new projective test that has become a strong competitor to the Rorschach Inkblots.

# About the Author

David Sheskin is a writer and artist whose work has been published extensively over the years. His short fiction and art have appeared in over 100 magazines including *The Dalhousie Review, Chicago Quarterly Review, The Satirist, Shenandoah, Puerto del Sol, The Florida Review and Quarterly West.* His art has also been published within the format of calendars (by Avalanche Publishing (*Folk Art by David Sheskin,* 1993) and Pomegranate Communications (*The Owl and the Pussycat* (2009, 2010, 2011) and *Puss and Boots* (2012)), as well as in calendars published in Europe (*Naïve Malerie,* 2004, 2005, 2006 by Ackermann in Germany), note cards, jigsaw puzzles, children's games and prints. Other books by David Sheskin are *Magician with a Pen* (Wingspan Press, 2007), *The Art of David Sheskin* (Wingspan Press, 2011), *Plaid Cats* (Wingspan Press, 2016), *Fraidy Cat* (Wingspan Press 2016), *Textures of Wildlife* (Wingspan Press, 2016), *Art That Speaks* (Wingspan Press, 2018), *David Sheskin's Art* (Wingspan Press, 2021) and *David Sheskin's Cabinet of Curiosities* (Wingspan Press, 2022).

www.ingramcontent.com/pod-product-compliance
Lightning Source LLC
Chambersburg PA
CBHW041100180526
45172CB00001B/38